Big STRIDES
in Letterland
by Lyn Wendon

A Visual System for Phonics in the Language of Childhood

Published by
Letterland Ltd
Barton, Cambridge CB3 7AY

Copyright © Lyn Wendon 1987–1994
ISBN 0 907345 28 X

First Printing 1987
Second Printing 1988
Third Printing 1990
Fourth Printing with revisions 1992
Fifth Printing 1994

Letterland was devised by Lyn Wendon and is part
of the Pictogram System copyright © Lyn Wendon 1973–1994
Letterland is a Registered Trade Mark.

Photography by Michael Little, Robin Hill and John Melton
Artwork by Jane Launchbury and Lyn Wendon
Cover and Page Design by Vicky Squires
Electronic Typesetting by Cambridge Photosetting Services
Printed and bound in Great Britain by
Raithby, Lawrence & Co. Ltd., Leicester & London

ACKNOWLEDGEMENTS

No system for teaching children can be better than the teacher who uses it. I have no doubt that the spread of Letterland owes much to the innumerable teachers everywhere who have chosen to become its citizens. My debt to them is great and continuing – for encouragement, for innovation and for feedback, and I take this opportunity to put it on record.

I also wish to thank Richard Carlisle who, a few years ago, first as parent and then as publisher, recognised the scope which Letterland might have beyond the classroom. Together with Jane Launchbury, an inspired book illustrator, he provided me with a visual model of how Letterland might be presented to the wider world.

Special appreciation is due to Doris Halls, who has sent every word of this volume through the word processor – many times. Without her care and patience I would not have seen the end of it in clean, crisp print, ready for the big printing presses.

L.W.

Contents

Introduction

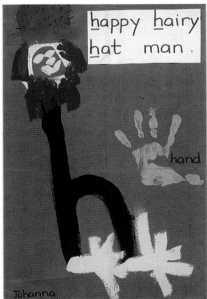

happy hairy hat man.

hand

Johanna
Waterbeach Primary School, Cambs.

A Little Bit of Theory

Educational theory on how to teach reading has always included hot debate over best methods. This controversy, broadly divided into phonics v.s. whole language, reached an almost warlike state in the late 1980's as 'whole language' teachers threw out reading schemes, abandoned phonics and flooded children with books of high literary merit but devoid of sufficient structure to help them to learn the alphabetic code.

Few teachers criticised the influx of children's literature, or the emphasis on constructing meaning from print. But many fought against the 'whole language' premise that phonic instruction was expendible.

This premise was based on the assumption that fluent readers' eyes flew over print without spelling-to-sound translation of every letter, deriving meaning instead by direct visual access. Beginner readers, they therefore assumed, could skip the elaborate decoding/encoding process while acquiring the same direct access to print.

Research has shown the rashness of this assumption: fluent readers only achieve such swift access to the extent that they have previously learned and overlearned the precise letter sequences in words. In fact, skilled readers continually rely on spelling-to-sound translation in the very complex act of deriving meaning from print.

Just consider for a moment how neadily a misprint can interrupt your own fluency as a skilled reader. The difference between the n and r *shape* is minimal. Yet your research for meaning is (readily) derailed by that tiny detail because the difference between the n and r *sound* is critical to meaning.

The concensus now is that we process print, the appearance, the pronunciation and the meaning of words, in three distinguishable activities:

- orthographic processing (of visual letter patterns)
- phonological processing (of sound-symbol correspondences)
- meaning/context processing (of the print message).

These activities do not precede each other. The act of reading consists of the *parallel* and *coinciding* activation of all three processes. Evidence points to all three being coordinated within the act of individual letter and letter cluster recognition. (1)

This coinciding of interdependent mental processes in response to print has important implications for the teaching of reading. Not only is phonic instruction re-instated, but its omission **at any time** in the course of the teaching of reading becomes a dereliction of responsibility to the children who are expecting to learn at our hands.

A child with too little phonic information is like a driver speeding along a road, oblivioius to traffic signs. Letters are signs. They signal. To leave a child without the means to decipher the signal system leads rapidly to errors and missed messages.

(1) (1990) Marilyn J Adams, BEGINNING TO READ, The M.I.T. Press, Cambridge, Mass.

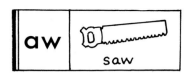

Old style phonic instruction. The link between **aw** and its sound is arbitrary. The information is of no intrinsic interest. There is no reason to explain the fact.

The Witch makes the apple taste **aw**ful.

Letterland mnemonics are integral to the letter shapes. The child's query, "But why a different sound?" has an answer, based on story logic, so the change becomes memorable.

A Little Bit of Sunshine

The next consideration is, how we may avoid the risk that a phonic emphasis in the teaching of reading will produce children whose attention is so riveted to the decoding process that they cannot attend to sentence or paragraph meaning? How, further, do we avoid the loss of motivation which so easily can cloud a rules and skills oriented phonic teaching programme?

The Letterland Programmes One and Two resolve both of these problems by introducing a mnemonic-aided pictogram alphabet, supported by stories about the animated letter characters. The stories carry the information which developing readers and spellers require. Programme Two in particular concentrates on the large number of phonic variables which arise when letters combine into new sounds.

The stories offer the children the very credible fiction that the Letterland characters live and are their secret friends. The pictograms serve to engage their interest and act as symbols of letter behaviour.

Enhanced Perception

Given that English is a virtual coral reef of many languages grown into one, youngsters have a great deal of information to learn about the symbol system in the first three years at school. Letterland enables them to do this in a friendly and playful context. They rapidly acquire a real discernment for the plain, black, abstract letter shapes and their functions by fusing (in their mind's eye as much as on paper) the animated characters of Letterland into them. Without altering the letter shapes in any way the pictograms alter children's *perception* of the letters. In the upshot, it is the Letterland characters which teach the children to register each word as uniquely readable.

Boredom does not exist in Letterland; curiosity does. Children like 'doing Letterland', not because they want to learn about phonics, but because they love hearing the story explanations and tracing the adventures of the Letterland characters in words.

As an example, compare the difference between teaching an unfamilar word by old-style phonic drill and by the Letterland route. In a word like **trawler**, the respective sound values of **a** and **w** shift for no apparent reason. Conventionally the child is taught: '**a** beside **w** makes the **aw** sound'. But there is nothing in this phonic fact to arrest a child's attention, nothing to help to integrate it functionally in his or her own word attack when meeting the **aw** pattern again. The sound/symbol link equation and the new picture (a saw or other familiar object) have no inherent connection.

By contrast, the Letterland pictogram and the accompanying anecdote supplies a 'reason' for the phonic rule. Any child of whatever ability will be alert to a witch (**w**) who turns back and makes an apple (**a**) taste a**w**ful, thereby causing the sound change. The story reason and picture fused into the letters make the new sound logical, dramatic, and therefore memorable.

Literally, Big Strides

The title of the first Letterland teacher's guide 'First Steps' underscores the fact that to know the alphabet is only to enter the foothills of literacy. In this second guide the routes are mapped for children to arrive rapidly at an overview of the written language in its entirety, all the oddities of English orthography notwithstanding!

By the Letterland route, you and the children explore the sound of letters within words more frequently for the purpose of writing the letters and words than for reading. In effect, you are establishing an *encoding emphasis designed primarily to inform spelling*. However, before the children know any difference, they will be finding that their emergent encoding knowledge has also become a *decoding skill which spontaneously informs their reading*.

All the new sounds which the original **a-z** letters create in combination are presented in this second stage as encounters between already familar Letterland characters, now interacting with each other in many words. Most children can comfortably complete both 'First Steps' and 'Big Strides' starting at five and finishing while they are still 7 years old.

Neither 'First Steps' nor 'Big Strides' attempt to cover all the skills that we wish children to acquire for full literacy. They concentrate instead on two important facets, namely

- **sound/symbol correspondences**
  the analysis and synthesis of letter strings

- **language development**
  both oral and written, listening and speaking skills, speculating, remembering, initiating and communicating ideas.

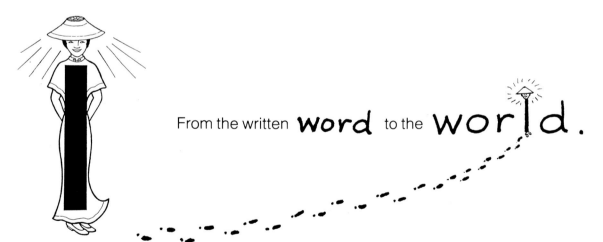

From the written **word** to the **world.**

Innovations

To achieve maximum progress within a minimum of time – and with pleasure – the following innovative strategies are main features of Letterland teaching.

New Name Tags for Letters Alliterative name tags rid you of dependence upon the time honoured but treacherous alphabet names 'Aee, Bee, Cee'; treacherous because they are so full of potential confusion. (See 'First Steps in Letterland' page 14: Your Instruction Language.)

Exclusion of Formal Rules and Technical Terms You use a minimum amount of instruction jargon. Instead of formally handing out facts you narrate stories which bring home the rules by analogy, entertaining while they inform.

Ideational Content for Sound/Symbol Teaching You give a *reason* for each new sound taught. There are no child oriented explanations in plain letter teaching to say why any particular letter or letter sequence should represent one particular sound rather than another.

Concept of Letters as Alive The fiction of human attributes within both small and capital letters makes it possible for children to identify them easily and even to identify with them.

Beachamwell Primary School, Norfolk.

Concept of the Reading Direction The pictogram designs all relate to the Reading Direction, so as to minimise reversals in both reading and writing. Design support for orientation is built into all reversible capital letter shapes as well as the small letter shapes.

Speedy Introduction of Digraphs Important digraphs such as **sh** are taught even before **a–z** are fully introduced. This practice ensures a flexible mental set in children's minds towards letter behaviour. An unproductive decoding-one letter-at-a-time approach (all too often associated with the early stages of phonic instruction) is thereby avoided.

Inclusion of Imaginative Thinking   Because you study letters as part of a fantasy world, children are encouraged to think imaginatively about letter behaviour.

Changes in Sound Are made Logical   Normally sounds made by letter clusters bear no logical relationship to single letter sounds. So the clusters may interfere with the children's understanding of the 'single' sounds. It is a fundamental principle that we learn the **unknown** best by relating it to the **known**. The Letterland Programme makes maximum use of this principle by explaining new cluster sounds through extensions of earlier stories about the single-letter sounds. Nothing needs to be 'unlearnt'. The stories draw seemingly chaotic spelling patterns into a coherent weave.

Ashcroft Infants, Tamworth, Staffs.

Re-useable Mnemonics   Traditional picture clues for sounds have no continuity, e.g. **c** for **c**ake, **h** for **h**orse but then **ch** for **ch**erries. By contrast the same pictogram mnemonics reappear for **c**, **h** and **ch**, coupled with a story which makes the otherwise arbitrary shift rational. The result is a reduction in the child's learning load.

Children as Animators   By adding picture details to the plain letter shapes each child utilises the empty spaces around the letters to inform his or her perception of the plain letters' shape, sound and orientation in space. The children's hand-drawn mnemonics encapsulate new learning, serving as swift reminders. Unlike sounds, their letter animation does not vanish as soon as the words have been pronounced.

Cherry Lane Infants, West Drayton, Middx.

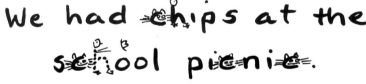

Terrington St. Clement Infants, Norfolk.

Five and six year olds in Cynthia Beckett's class, Callowbrook First School, Rubery, Birmingham.

11

Bradley Barton Primary, Newton Abbot, Devon.

Hayes Park Infants, Hayes, Middlesex.

Bradley Barton Primary, Devon. Part of an original Letterland musical involving all 160 children.

Children as Enactors of Letter Behaviour   By impersonating the letter characters, as well as imitating their sounds, the children experience whole-body involvement (high kinaesthetic input) to accompany their sound/symbol learning. They also maximise visual and auditory input when they sequence themselves in rows to demonstrate, big as life, numerous changes in sound.

A 'Lie Fallow' Concept   Much of the initial Letterland teaching, through oral work, singing, and play-acting is conducted as an end in itself. At first you can treat any factual learning as a spin-off from that activity. You lead the children to discover for themselves how the information they are acquiring happens to have relevance to reading and spelling.

St. Ninian's Episcopal School, Perth, Scotland

Eileen Gallacher's class of juniors acting out the **kn** story for the infant classes.

Use of Curiosity to Determine the Teaching Order   The sequence of presentation used for this book is *not* a mandatory teaching order. Children are surrounded by words. If any one word arouses their curiosity (unless it is totally irregular) there is no need to postpone the relevant story which gives the *reason* for the new sound. Because the original mnemonics remain valid, earlier facts are reinforced even as you tell the story for the new sound. So your teaching order can be highly flexible.

Friendliness Factor   Curiosity is enhanced by a 'friendliness factor'. The Letterland characters become the children's friends; so when they change their behaviour the children really want to know why.

Hayes Park Infants, Hayes, Middlesex

Picture Coding

The Alphabet is a Code

The alphabet is a child's first introduction to a coded system of communication. The teacher's dilemma is the complexity of its structure. To teach one sound for each symbol fails to explain that nearly every letter has more than one sound-function, dictated by the letter's position in a very particular sequence. Pictograms bridge this dilemma.

Picture Coding: Starter Pack

Each pictogram incorporates in its letter a character which serves as both a visual and auditory clue to its identity. The children learn the unfamiliar letter-shapes through the familiar character-shapes. They find the single letter sounds simply by starting to name the pictogram character which a plain letter resembles. They become aware of slight but critical differences in curve or length of line (e.g. **n/h**, **a/d**, **a/u**, **m/n**, **v/w**, **i/l**, **h/k**) by contrasting not only the *plain* letter shapes but also the parallel *pictogram* shapes.

Each pictogram depicts a character looking, moving or pointing in the reading and writing direction to minimise confusion between similar letters (e.g. **b/d**, **b/p**, **p/q/g**, **f/t**, **M/W**, **n/u**, **s/z**, **H/N**). By adding pictogram details ('picture coding' the letters) the children confirm for themselves the special properties of each letter.

Picture Coding: Main Pack

As the children progress, their more advanced picture coding helps them to record their own learning. Each drawing holds an otherwise fleeting sound before their eyes. The letters are made to 'speak', with the child's own hand ensuring that they really do signify as sounds. The drawings also enable you to check at a glance whether or not they have illustrated the sounds correctly.

Both you and the children drop the coding as soon as the pictogram props are no longer needed. This usually happens at about the same time as the novelty of adding the picture coding wears off.

Bridgtown Infants, Cannock, Staffs.

I know that she knew.

Judy Manson's class recounting and acting out the **ew** story, Callowbrook First School, Rubery, Birmingham.

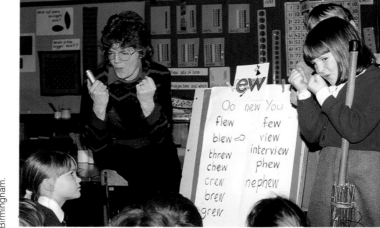

apricot

apricot

broom

broom

colour

color

Regional Pronunciation

The picture coded examples in this guide assume standard English pronunciation. Where regional or individual pronunciation differs the picture code is adaptable. For example, either illustration of the words **apricot** and **broom** might be correct, depending upon their pronunciation by the person who is adding the picture coding. You can also adapt your coding where, for example, U.K. and U.S.A. spelling conventions differ, as in words like **colour** and **color**.

In a few cases teachers may prefer to exclude a pictogram as inapplicable in a particular area, e.g. Vowel Stealer pictograms in Scotland, where the pronunciation of **ar**, **er**, **ir**, **or**, and **ur** is scarcely different from the single letter sounds.

Where there is no correspondence between particular letters and their normal sounds, either because of idiosyncracies in English spelling or because of regional or individual pronunciation you draw a box round the relevant letters. In these cases the box signals the disparity. See 'The Use of Boxes' p.30.

Unaccented Syllables

There are in everyone's speech patterns unaccented syllables where a sound is 'swallowed'. The most common sound in an unaccented syllable is the 'schwa' sound, usually an **i** sound (as in **i**nk) or an **u** sound (as in **u**mbrella): 'inventid'/ invented, 'churchis'/churches, 'animul'/animal, 'delivud'/ delivered.

If the pictograms were used to indicate this 'schwa' sound in all these unaccented syllables a vast number of syllables would have to be illustrated with **i**nk bottles or **u**mbrellas, regardless of the actual spelling of the words. Clearly this would undercut the purpose of the pictograms. They are not primarily a pronunciation guide. They are a decoding device for reading and an aid to accuracy in spelling.

Part of an original Letterland play devised by Pauline Rowse and Jacqueline Prouse, teaching at Bradley Barton Primary, Newton Abbot, Devon.

The Materials

Programme One

Programme One for Letterland covers the shape and the sound of both small and capital letters plus the first important digraphs **sh**, **wh**, **ing**, **ang**, **ong** and short and long vowels. It introduces children to the strategies of word building by means of story telling, play-acting, reading and writing. The teaching progression of Programme One is more structured than the materials in Programme Two, when the children have acquired confidence in letter behaviour.

The 'First Steps' pack has the following components:
- The 'First Steps' Teacher Guide, 160 pages, plus Scope and Sequence Charts No. 1 and No. 2.
- Letterland Wall Frieze (both small and capital letters)
- Songbook and Audio Tape One.
- Large Pictograms **a-z** Photocopy Masters.
- Large Pictograms **A-Z** Photocopy Masters.
- 50 Picture Code Cards.
- 26 'Listen and Write' Photocopy Masters.
- 36 'Code Sheet' Photocopy Masters.
- 24 Consonant Capers Photocopy Masters.
- Peel-Off Stickers for **a-z**.

The 50 Picture Code Cards and the 36 'Code Sheet' Photocopy Masters (illustrated on the next page) are useful with both Packs.

Other Resources

These resources can all be used to consolidate Programme One teaching and/or serve to initiate newcomers to Letterland in a class where some have been taught Programme One but others have not.

- 40 **Letterland Link Early Readers** for the enjoyment of Letterland without any obvious teaching. They bridge school and home.
- **Letterland Picture Dictionary.**
- **Letterland on Micro** (for BBC, Nimbus, Archimedes).
- **Letterland Early Authors** (Overlays for Concept Keyboard and stories for children to generate).
- **Storybook Early Authors** (Overlays and stories based on books pictured below).
- 32 **Letterland Finger Puppets** (use in both Programmes).

Other items not illustrated here include:
- **Cursive Poster** and handwriting photocopy masters
- **Letterland Shuffle** (card game: sentence making and punctuation).
- **Word Hunts** (Crossword photocopy masters for all levels of ability).

The Letterland ABC and Storybooks (left)
- The **ABC** describes each one of the Letterland characters with a liberal use of alliterative words and objects to discover within the illustrations.
- The **Storybooks**. The Channel 4 TV series called 'Adventures Letterland' is based on 12 of them.

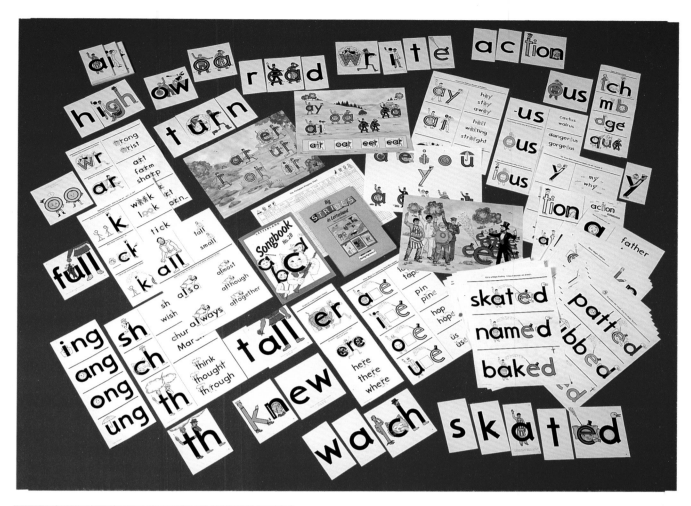

Whitehouse Common First School, Birmingham.

The 'Big Strides' pack has four components:

- 'Big Strides' Teachers Guide, 160 pages, plus Progress Chart for 35 pupils.

- 79 Picture Code Cards.

- Songbook and Audio Tape 2B with 25 songs to support and playfully extend your teaching of numerous spelling patterns.

- 4 full colour Vowel Scenes and 49 Display Charts. For full information on how best to make use of the Scenes and Charts, turn to pages 20–25.

The stories and general information in this pack cover all essential word structure in the English language. By using the Picture Code Cards from both packs children can set out any word with a recurring spelling pattern. Plain sides up for easy parts. Pictogram sides for difficult parts.

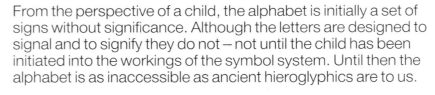

Teacher/Parent/Child Triangle

From the perspective of a child, the alphabet is initially a set of signs without significance. Although the letters are designed to signal and to signify they do not – not until the child has been initiated into the workings of the symbol system. Until then the alphabet is as inaccessible as ancient hieroglyphics are to us.

From the perspective of adults – teachers and parents – the problem is how to explain the intricacies of our alphabetical system in a way which children can appreciate and *will want to hear*.

The introduction of an imaginary place called 'Letterland' has provided a fresh solution to this communication problem, because Letterland is a place of childhood. At the same time it is the location of all that needs to be known about the alphabet letter names, about correct letter formation, about the phonic system of spelling-sound translation, and the rules of word structure. All this information is carried in the form of brief stories about letter characters who inhabit Letterland. For example, the different sounds of **a** in words like **pat**, **part** and **paw** are given 'reasons' in story form in the place of abstract, unreasoned, rules.

An important result of this new, narrative form of instruction (which sprang in the first instance from children) is that they can speak the instruction language themselves from the outset. Simply by sharing with each other the latest story, or reminding a friend of an earlier one, they can even instruct each other.

Every teacher has experienced how the need to teach any new subject galvanises their own learning of that subject. Letterland provides teachers and parents with an opportunity whereby together they can give children this same beneficial experience.

This is how it works.

You brief the parents, in gradual stages, about the Letterland characters and inter-connecting stories. **Reading and Writing with Letterland**, a Parent's Guide by Judy Manson (published 1992) is useful to this end.

You explain to the parents that animating letters has a unique effect on children. Even 3, 4 and 5 year olds can learn the abstract symbols just as easily as their older brothers and sisters, simply by scribbling the pictogram character details on to letters, written boldly for them by a parent. The parents learn, not to teach their children what they learnt about Letterland, but to encourage the *children to teach them*. Each time their child comes home with a little something to tell about Letterland (a new character in Letterland, how to animate the new letter, or to share a little story or a Letterland rhyme or song) the parent is in an informed position to support the new learning.

The most subtle and effective approach to Programme Two involves the child coming home from school and showing his or her parents how to picture code, say, Giant All in **all**, **tall**, **small** and **also** and sharing the story explanations. The parent by lending a willing ear and maintaining good eye contact responds as a *learner*. She/he is impressed, shows it, and looks forward to the next story and next picture coding. This parental listening role ensures that the school and home stay synchronised over the timing of new sounds to be learnt, and allows the children to move into the novel and exciting position of teaching their parents for a change!

Throughout their early years children are bound to experience most of their learning at the hands of those who know better than they do. They are always the passive receivers of adult input.

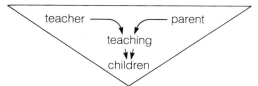

Within the context of Letterland the dynamics shift in favour of the child, who becomes a more active contributor in the triangle.

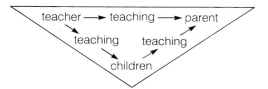

The role reversal of the 'child in the know' and the parent as 'the willing learner' can do wonders for a child's self-esteem. At the same time the parent becomes a good role model by daily demonstrating an interested learning attitude at the child's hands. Another equally important benefit: the child's oral language skills —so often atrophied by the TV age they live in — are given scope to expand.

Home/School Link materials to enable parents to provide informed support to Letterland teaching at school. ⟶

How to use this Book

Teaching Order At first you may prefer to follow roughly the order of presentation in this guide. Before long, however, you should feel free to choose your own order as your children's interest and needs dictate. This Programme Two is designed to make any type of word structure equidistant from a centre point. *That point is where you are standing at any given moment in the reading curriculum.*

This second stage can be introduced without prior use of Programme One, but it does assume that you have access to the Picture Code Cards from Programme One for building words which both you and the children will construct and discuss.

Any difficult or advanced word structure can be dealt with by 'boxing' the relevant cluster of letters and by promising a story explanation later. (See page 30 for the 'boxing' routine.)

Teach Spelling and Reading Together Good readers are often high visualisers. Spelling for them involves no special or separate skill. They can generally 'call up' words on their own mental 'screen' and copy. But poor readers are often low visualisers. They cannot refer to that mental 'screen'; or at least they cannot rely on it. They must reverse the reading process (which goes from symbol to sound) and spell 'by ear'.

Throughout this book there is an emphasis on the sound value of letters and letter combinations. No child is a perfect visualiser and English plays tricks. We all need to know how to move effectively from speech to written symbol. Letterland aims to cater particularly for that need.

George Palmer Infants, Reading, Berks

Display Charts With 49 charts available the order of presentation is for you to decide. The groupings illustrated on the next pages are only one set of possibilities. Ideally the displays become interactive, with the children often bringing new examples to add because they enjoy discovering their Letterland friends within words.

Parents working with their children during one of Lees Hill Infant School's weekly Reading Workshops, Barnsley, W. Yorks. The parents have tea and a ten-minute briefing by Carol Lycett, Head Teacher, before each session.

Chart Display Suggestions

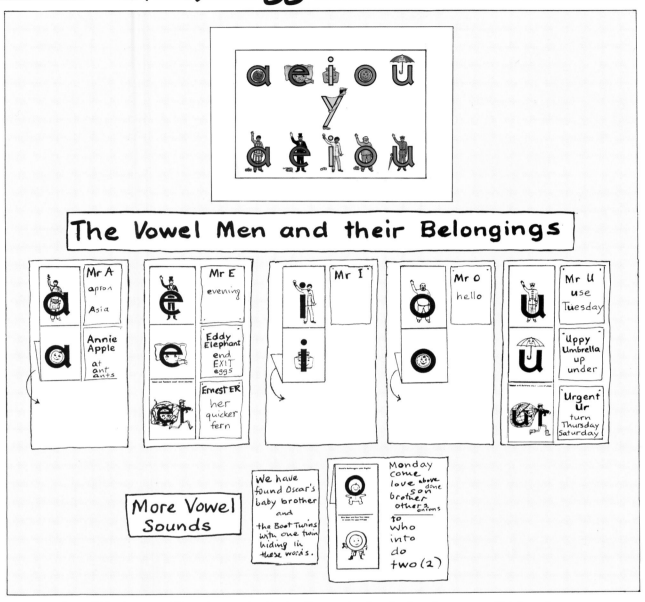

The Vowel Men and their Belongings

More Vowel Sounds

We have found Oscar's baby brother and the Boot Twins with one twin hiding in these words.

Monday come love above done son brother others onions to who into do two (2)

You will find many different ways to display these charts, singly or in groups. Fold any less relevant section out of sight until needed (**ar**, **er**, **ir**, **or**, **ur**: see also page 23). Keep the display 'alive' by changing the examples frequently. Or, make any one chart a focal point where the children collect words of a kind.

The Hat Man Stories

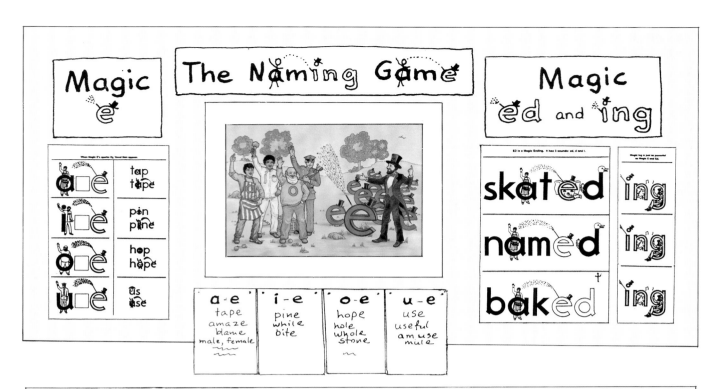

See pages 49-51 before displaying the double consonant charts.

The Vowel Stealers

The above display shows the ringleader, Robber Red, in control of the Witch in **wr**, and his gang of 5 Vowel Stealers at work. Another suggestion. Place the right hand chart under the left one, place a long scroll to the right, and invite children to add as many words of each kind as they can find. First take guesstimates 'Which robber does the most vowel stealing of the notorious five?' 'Who will come next? And next? Next? Last?'

This display highlights important recurring spelling patterns and key examples. You may like to put children in charge of changing the examples every week.

Vowel Men Out Walking
the First One Does the Talking

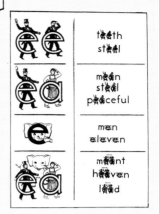

Who goes out walking MOST in words?

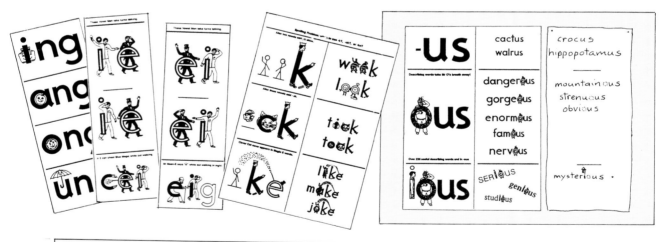

ay	ai	oa	ee	ea	ea
hay today	hail daily	foam toast boat oats	speed greedy sleep	Let's read it now at least creased creature beat beast clean, wheat reason	I read it then. ready head meadow heavy weather

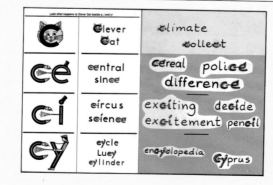

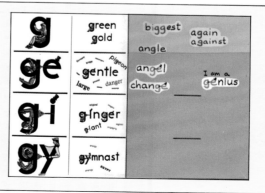

24

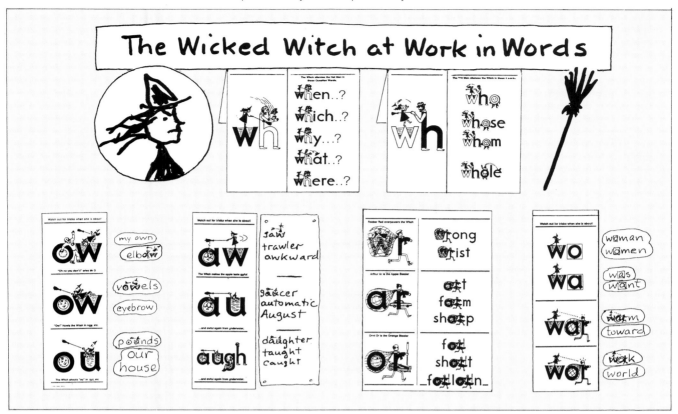

The Wicked Witch at Work in Words

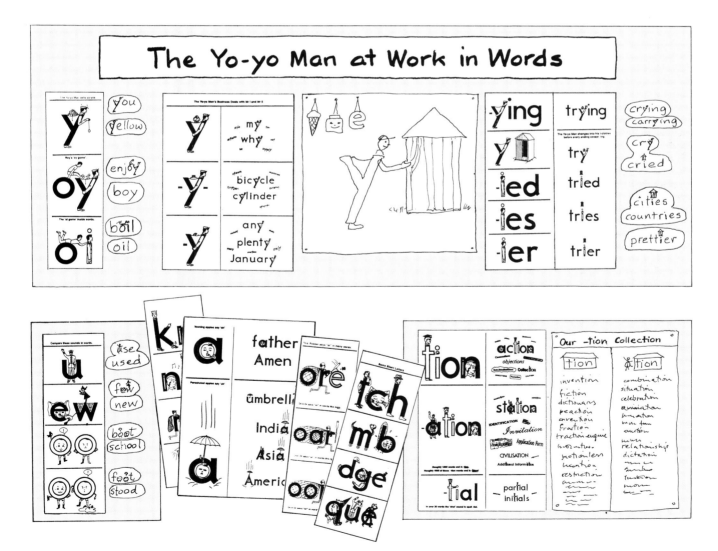

The Yo-yo Man at Work in Words

Questions and Answers

The Reading Direction

Letterland and Reading Schemes

Question   Will Letterland fit in with our particular reading scheme?

Answer   There is an ever widening range of reading schemes available. Years of experience by many teachers has shown that, no matter which scheme(s) a school prefers, the *parallel* introduction of Letterland makes for swifter progress.

Similarly, schools which prefer only non-scheme books report that Letterland provides a sense of structure and initial confidence which could otherwise be lacking where a school relies exclusively on non-scheme books.

Design your reading time to encourage sentence fluency and sight word skills. While reading, a child should concentrate on the message of the story, using syntax and contextual clues for meaning. Ideally you provide difficult words immediately and do not interrupt in order to analyse the medium. Instead your Letterland lessons provide the time for showing just how the parts make up the whole. You can be sure that every *one* bit of Letterland lore will open up hundreds and even thousands of words to phonic attack. It is a source of tremendous confidence for the children to crack the code. It can also take literally years off the time it takes for them to become fluent readers and confident spellers.

Where Do I Begin?

Question   My children already know **a–z** as plain letter shapes. Some know their sounds, too, but know nothing of Letterland. Where do I begin in this MAIN PACK?

Answer   Try following these three steps first.

● Use the Starter Pack Picture Code Cards to introduce all the Letterland characters one by one. Give their character names and their sounds. Add story details from the 'First Steps' Teacher's Guide if appropriate. This adds motivation but is not essential at this stage. You can even introduce **a–z** all in one sitting since only the character names are entirely new. (The character names are available on page 42 in the 'Motivate to Punctuate' section.)

● Explain that for any *sound* the children cannot remember they should *start* to say the Letterland character's name. They will find the correct sound right there on their lips! (Give practice as necessary.)

● The next day see how many character names they can remember. Revise their pronunciation of the sounds. Don't accept 'cuh, fuh, huh, kuh, luh, muh, nuh, puh, suh, tuh, or 'zuh' as correct. Use the Letterland Singsongs for **a–z**, and the Consonant Capers' Songbook and Audio Tape 2A if consonant blends are causing difficulty.

Next feel free to teach any story you judge appropriate in this book.

Betty Griffith's class, a school play, Boney Hay First, Walsall.

Here are the offenders:

C – *see*	Q – *cue*
F – *ef*	R – *are*
G – *jee*	S – *es*
H – *aitch*	U – *you*
K – *cay*	W– *double-you*
L – *el*	X – *ex*
M – *em*	Y – *why*
N – *en*	

Philip O'Neill teaching at Fleming Fulton School for the Physically Handicapped, Belfast, Ireland.

Why 'Annie Apple' etc. Instead of 'Aee, Bee, Cee'?

Question   My children are already used to calling the letters 'aee, bee, cee,' etc. Do I need to encourage them use the Letterland character names 'Annie Apple', etc. all the time instead?

Answer   No, but bear in mind the following three points:

● 15 of the 21 consonant names actually begin with another letter's sound (e.g. **c**-*see*, **s**-*es*). Check whether this is a source of confusion in reading or spelling mistakes among your particular pupils.

● If they are still uncertain of some **a** -**z** single sounds you should realise that your continued use of the traditional consonant names will actually deprive both *you* and *them* of new opportunities to reinforce all consonants sounds. By contrast, daily use of the Letterland character names means they will always find the correct sound at the start of *every* character name.

● The 5 vowel names give no clue to the 5 vowel sounds. By talking about Annie Apple, Eddy Elephant, etc. for *short* vowels and Mr A, Mr E, etc. for *long* vowels both you and the children can communicate without ambiguity about both.

If you prefer to talk about the **c**at, the **d**uck, the **e**lephant, the **f**ireman, etc., instead of 'Clever Cat', 'Dippy Duck' etc. feel free to do so. (The only letters which do not yield easily to this approach are **b**, **n** and **t**. In these cases just shorten their alliterative names to Ben, Nick and Tom.)

Some teachers like to maintain the '**a**ee, **b**ee, **c**ee' terms but lapse into Letterland names mainly to tell the stories and to clarify spelling mistakes. Others prefer to use the Letterland names exclusively because they find the children are more likely to stay 'tuned in' while they instruct. The children will also talk about letters spontaneously with you and among themselves in ways they would never have reason to talk about the '**a**ee, **b**ee, **c**ee'!

Question   Assuming I go whole-heartedly for using the Letterland character names, when and how do I make the transition to the traditional **a**ee, **b**ee, **c**ee?

Answer   The likelihood is that you will never need to. Most teachers find children pick them up by themselves.

Won't I Confuse the Children?

Question   Is there a risk that Letterland stories will interfere with other stories that children read?

Answer   Usually your best opener for telling a new Letterland story will be when children need to *spell* rather than *read* a new word, so that distinguishing between the recurring little Letterland fables and real story plots does not cause a problem to them.

Bridgtown C. Primary, Cannock.

Pembridge Hall Infants, London.

Merland Rise First, Epsom, Surrey.

Book written by two 10 yr olds in their free time.
Pinkwell Jr School, Hayes, Middx.

You may find it useful to cue a hesitating child with a Letterland reference during reading, by pointing quickly to the relevant Flap Chart. Or you may provide a quick verbal reminder of a Letterland anecdote or song. But *not* if this means that the child loses the author's message. Make a mental note of the difficult word and look into its structure in a later Letterland lesson.

Help! They know More than I do!

Question   What should I do if the class I will take this year knows more about Letterland than I do? Do I need to read all 160 pages of the 'First Steps in Letterland' teacher's guide even before I start on this 'Big Strides' guide?

Answer   If the 'First Steps' guide is available do read Section One (pages 9-21) and study the Scope and Sequence Charts so that you will have a rough idea what ground the children have already covered. Study the Code Sheets too, if possible. Then try this suggestion. Create an opportunity for the children to change roles. Let *them* teach *you* all they know about **a –z**. Observe their language as they instruct you. Their story-retelling will give you the foundations on which you will be building as *you* tell them the next 'Big Strides' stories. If you do start off with this role-reversal the result will be

* a child-initiated revision accomplished,
* an opportunity provided for new children to learn from their peers,
* a new tone set by you.

Your Letterland sessions will be enhanced by the children's awareness that you will not be their drill sergeant in a rigorous march to literacy but rather their travelling companion on a shared journey of discovery in the land of words.

'Language Experience' Teaching

Question   Is Letterland compatible with 'Language Experience' approach?

Answer   Yes, indeed, Letterland places the same emphasis on children's own language. You write their wording beside paintings, objects of interest, etc. You also act as scribe for their own stories. In addition, when they copy your handwriting you picture code chosen letters for them.

I went to a big party.

You thereby ensure that they do not copy unthinkingly, and you give them confidence in learning so many otherwise abstract symbols.

Special Needs Teaching

Question   Where do I begin with special needs children?

Answer   You do not have to introduce **a -z** first. As mentioned above, this could make your pupils feel you think that they know nothing. The only characters they need to 'meet' may be ones which give rise to mistakes **b/d/p/q** or **c/s/z, e/i, g/j,** for

example. Introduce each one at a moment of need to help them with their mistakes. Then the whimsy of Letterland will be more welcome. Introduce the **a**pple letter, for example, only briefly before teaching about 'what happens to the **a**pple' in words like c**a**r, or s**a**w, or t**a**ll (pages 109, 138 and 99 respectively.)

No Books at First

Question What do I do with children who hate all books because they are associated too closely with failure?

Answer Some children simply cannot cope with a string of words and at the same time attend to sentence meaning; that is to say, not until they have gained some confidence in cracking the code. Right now too many words trip them up. Try a new tack. Just tell them a few Letterland stories. After each one, have the children picture code the two example sentences that follow the story. Then plaster those sentences around your classroom walls. Re-read them together. The coding will ensure attention to the structure as well as to general whole-word shapes. Since all the sentences are relatively short the added burden of trying to focus on overall meaning is removed. As their skill in phonic attack grows try short paragraphs on any topic of special interest. Soon books will be a manageable goal.

Plastic Pockets

Select words and phrases. Insert them in plastic pockets. Have the children add the picture-coding (use non permanent overhead projector pens) whenever they feel the need for picture support. They read the words, (tick), wipe off the coding and if they can re-read them without help turn your tick into a star! Finally, wipe off all stars and check in a later lesson whether all words remain manageable – worthy of stars again!

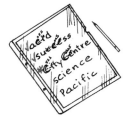

This work on single words and short phrases will have the further advantage of allowing time to strengthen awareness as to why many words are spelt as they are. Move on to coding sentences as described above. Then on to single, short paragraphs before providing completely fresh books, not associated with earlier failure.

Letterland Teaching Routines

The Letterland approach offers a number of teaching routines, as parallel activities to reading, which would not be available in 'plain letter' teaching. Use them as needed.

The Picture Coding Routine

Include some picture coding as a regular feature for each new sound you teach. It will enable you to progress more swiftly.

Animating letters consolidates a child's memory for a particular sound. Adding head and feet, or ears, eyes and whiskers, etc. only takes a few easy pencil strokes. Hey presto! The inanimate symbols come to life! (See also 'Picture Coding' page 13).

Each Letterland story is followed by a handwritten picture coded sentence plus two more arrowed sentences for picture coding in class.

> Picture code each
> **o and oa**

1. He loaded the old boat with coal.
2. That goat is fond of hot toast!

hot toast

While the children may have the impression that all they have to do is to decorate some letters, in fact they are doing much more. In order to add the picture code to any given letters each child must:

i.   *read* the sentence, (with help if necessary),
ii. *re-read* each word (providing repetition with a purpose),
iii. *listen* to their own pronunciation of each word, carefully enough to pick out the sounds made by the specific letters to be picture coded,
iv. *relate* these sounds to the correct pictogram,
v.   *confirm* the letter sounds in picture form.

The Use of Boxes

Boxes are an interim device for you to signal a letter combination which has yet to be taught which does not conform to earlier information. Many sound shifts will be explained by a pictogram story in due course, but for the time being your boxes will save fruitless decoding attempts and alert the child to look at whole word shapes and for context and syntax clues.

Similarly, show the children how to use boxes when they are coding words for themselves. They cannot afford, for example, to code an **a** by drawing an apple if they cannot hear its **ă** sound. Instead they use a box to show that they have discovered an irregular word.

Jane
Martha
Barbara
Richard
Catherine
Paul
Louise
Sean

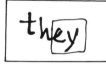

many

they

they

e

Make Use of Children's Names

Names carry motivational strength and are frequently used in writing. They are therefore, especially at the start, valuable for illustrating letter behaviour. Some names are excellent examples of 'Magic **e**'; James, Jane, Hope. Others like Martha, Charles help teach the **ar** sound, etc.

Holding imaginary walkie-talkies the children play-act the **ar** sound. Graham Holbrow, Headmaster, Hatherleigh Primary School, Devon.

However, many names will contain irregularities or sounds which you have not yet taught. Draw a box around any difficult group of letters or sounds which you do not wish to teach yet and promise a story later. A few children, with names like Louise or Sean, may be disappointed to be offered no story; invite them, in due course, to think up their own 'one-off' little stories to explain the letter behaviour in their boxes. (Many examples of coded names can be found in 'First Steps'.)

'Wonky Words' Collection

Difficult words like **any** and **many** and **they** are good candidates for a 'Wonky Word' Collection. (Use another name if you prefer.) Have children write them on cards, adding boxes themselves.

From time to time, revise the collection to see which words can come out because now there is some Letterland logic and picture coding to explain the boxed sound, e.g.Mr Mean-E sounding like an **a** in th**e**y.

Story-Retelling

Few children enjoy repeating rules, but many like retelling little anecdotes. Recounting is an important part of language development. Retelling stories also provides a valuable form of revision and consolidation of information gained. Make narrating *by the children* a brief but regular feature of your Letterland sessions.

Dressing Up

Visualise six children crowding around a Letterland Costume Box. You overhear them saying: 'I'll be the Hairy Hat Man. You be Poor Peter.' 'I'm going to be the Kicking King' 'Then I'll be the Queen with her umbrella.' 'O.K, then. Give me that mask. I'll

Merland Rise First, Epsom, Surrey.

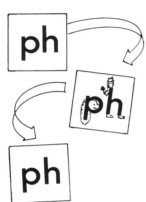

be Robber Red and Jan can be the Wicked Witch.' The six children then don tabards or headbands and other identifying props. Then they all dash around the playground. How old are these children? They are a new group of rising five year olds, in school for only five weeks. They have not yet studied the **h, k, qu, p, r, w** sounds, not to mention **ph** or **wr**. They have just picked up the Letterland names from the older children simply because they wanted to wear the props and be like their older peers as they saw them dressing up in free play time.

Their learning is incidental. But seeds have been sown. These will sprout when the children start to need to know. Meanwhile a genuine interest in letters has already been established, without any teaching! Provide enough props for this incidental learning to thrive. The children or parents can make many of the props. See also 'Taking Letterland Beyond the Written Page' (page 35).

Quick Charades

Two or more children mime a Letterland character without props or letters, e.g. **mb**. (They should only add sound if the miming is not sufficient to identify the letter). The other children must guess who, and then quickly think of as many words as possible with **-mb** in them. (With practice they will be able to list quite a few.)

Visual Memory Training

To make plain letter(s) cue their own sounds use the following routine.
* Hold up the plain letter side of a Picture Code Card.
* Quickly flash the pictogram side and return to plain side.
* Ask children to describe what they saw.
* Have them retell the relevant story in their own words.
* Follow up by picture coding some examples.

Callowbrook First, Rubery, Birmingham.

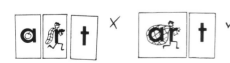

Linking Words of a Kind

Give out words of a kind, e.g. **ow**l, cr**ow**n, br**ow**n, fl**ow**er, cl**ow**n, sh**ow**er, t**ow**el, v**ow**el men. Ask the children to think up sentences using these words. This is more effective than simply memorising 'word families'. Younger children can paint some of these objects around their own **ow** pictogram and then label the objects.

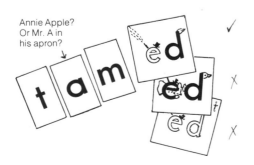

Annie Apple? Or Mr. A in his apron?

Guessing Games

There are many possibilities. For example, set out several words, with most letters plain side up. Ask, what picture do you think will be on the other side?

Vary the game by deliberately choosing some wrong cards, so that the children can spot the mistakes.

Then ask what picture *should* be on the other side to show the right sound.

32

Make Tape Recordings

Encourage language from reticent children by tape recording them, whispering like the Hairy Hat Man, hissing like Sammy Snake, pouting and making sad little 'p ...' sounds like Poor Peter, munching and saying 'Mmmm' like Munching Mike or impersonating the Wicked Water Witch crying 'Wwwatch out, I'm the Wwwicked Wwwater Wwwitch!' and so on. Let them choose 'who to be' and what to say when they meet each other (on the tape) as Letterland characters. Some children will enjoy writing parts for themselves.

Stress liveliness of expression and encourage practice to reach fluency. It will make the final recording really good listening - and provide just the confidence boost which some children need.

Spelling Pictures

Choose words where children can illustrate both the picture coding *and* the whole word meaning. A collection of these Spelling Pictures bound into a book can become a special kind of classroom resource, a unique picture dictionary made, alphabetised and indexed by the children.

Parent Involvement

First, see page 15 'The Teacher/Parent/Child Triangle'. Most parents are intrigued to learn about Letterland lore. They only need to keep a story or two ahead of the children whom you assign them to help. Because no technical teaching jargon is involved or 'rule talk' they quickly move into a position to be highly supportive of your Letterland programme.

Peer Tutoring

If you appoint older readers, say 7 or 8 year olds to assist the little ones, the opportunity arises to revise bits of Letterland logic with the *peer-tutors first*, to the ultimate benefit of both the peer-tutors and tutees. For example, if the story a tutee will be reading includes *knights* then the **kn** pictogram will be relevant. During reading the peer-tutor should provide the whole word, knight, so as not to interrupt the flow of the story. But *after* the story, the peer-tutor can help the younger child construct the word **knight** on the Picture Code Cards, retell the **kn** story and show how to make a Spelling Picture which illustrates both the **kn** pictogram and the whole-word meaning of **knights**.

Creative Writing

Because Letterland is an imaginary place there is scope for all sorts of creative writing.

● Have the children choose from an early-level dictionary as many useful words as possible to include in a story about a favourite character, e.g. for the Hairy Hat Man; **hunting, hut, helicopter, hippopotamus, hospital.** The chosen words help the child to think of a plot.

● Write letters to the Letterland characters. Make up addresses for them. 'Post' the letters to classmates. They reply in the style which they imagine the characters themselves might use.

● Describe/invent

 • a special machine for getting to Letterland,

 • possible houses for favourite Letterland characters (some ideas from a group of 5 year olds for Jumping Jim: a **j**elly house, a **j**igsaw house, a **j**umping house, a **j**igsaw house on a **j**elly hill, a **j**ellybean house).

 • favourite pastimes for various characters: Bouncy Ben **b**lowing **b**ubbles, **b**uilding **b**ridges with **b**locks.

 • design Christmas cards picturing presents for Letterland inhabitants (example – a 6 year old's idea for the Hairy Hat Man – a **h**umming bird with only a very little **h**um because he **h**ates noise).

● Suggest that the children describe a trip to Letterland, who they meet, what they say to the various characters, how the characters might reply and what adventures they might have together, etc.

● Let the children flesh out any aspect of the Letterland characters' lives they like. The result may be semi-autobiographic, e.g.

> The Kicking King got hit in the tummy by a football and fell in the mud and his Mummy had to change his clothes!

Fine! This 5 year old has already understood how a novelist transposes personal experience on to fictitious characters!

Letterland Plays

Some schools enjoy devising their own original plays based on Letterland. Their plots incorporate songs from the Letterland songbooks and Audio Tapes, snatches of Letterland lore and their own ideas for adventures in Letterland. Christmas in Letterland, for example, can combine a seasonal theme with a light-hearted instructional element.

Letterland Across the Curriculum

Taking Letters Beyond the Written Page

In play-acting letters can become something more than flat marks on a flat page. Giving them a third dimension brings them within the children's control. Many of them can also make good themes for music and movement. As the children explore ways to express any letter-character in movement they repeat its sound. Even a simple Apple Dance can be visually striking, perhaps with huge paper apples to wield as part of the movement. Other groups of letters can come in to culminate the dance by forming whole words.

At the simplest level of letter 'impersonation', children can appear as **a** -**z**, each wearing a letter and perhaps a bit of costume. They carry cards showing three words, entering one by one on the audience's left.

1st Child: Hello. I am Mr A, the Apron Man. I say my name 'A', in words like **apron** and **acorn** and **ape**. Here in Letterland I grow whole orchards full of **a**pples, too. Here comes one of them.'

2nd Child: I am one of Mr A's **a**ppetising **a**pples. The sound I make in words is 'ă. .ă. .ă. .' like in **apple** and **arrow** and **axe.**

3rd Child: I am Bouncy Ben. I bounce along in words like this. (Bounces to right, arms held high for ears.) The sound I make in words is '**b**. .**b**. . **b**. .', like in **blue** and **ball** and in my name, **Bouncy Ben**. (And so on. The audience can be invited to join in reading the words, so the child becomes a little master of ceremonies for the whole gathering.)

With 26 characters and 5 Vowel Men there are enough parts for 31 children. If the class is bigger, several children can be Silent **e**'s. They hold big red **e**'s, carry wands, and say nothing. When asked why not, they shake their heads silently. Mr E then steps up and explains proudly that they are his special Silent Magic **e**'s which always work silently in words.

A more ambitious assembly can be planned around a series of words like **tap**, **tape**, etc. acting and singing about the Magic E principle, and perhaps the Vowels Out Walking principle (Letterland Songbook 2B). As children progress, the possibilities for acting out word structure increase daily.

Act out Digraphs

Once children have play-acted in a little Letterland story it is difficult for them to forget how those letters behave in words. The imitation pattern creates the memory pattern.

Once you have told the **ch** story, for example, half of the class can become Clever Cats, making voiceless 'c...' sounds. They move about enacting words beginning with **c**, e.g. **c**url up in a **c**orner, **c**law imaginary **c**arpets, **c**limb about, **c**lean themselves, **c**opy each other (**c**opy **c**ats), or **c**reep and **c**rawl to **c**atch a mouse. The other half of the class might become Hat Men whispering '**hhh**' as they **h**urry or **h**op. At a given point each Hat Man approaches a **c**at. The moment he touches that **c**at they both 'sneeze'. When the hall is full of **ch** sounds you signal to the pairs to separate. They immediately revert to their separate sounds as they move apart.

Use the same approach for acting out other sounds.

The two sounds of **wh** allow for lots of imaginary **wh**acking and protest gestures. Each Witch recites the five Question Words starting with **wh** as she **wh**acks the Hat Man's imaginary hat off. Each Hat Man shouts, '**Wh**o do you think you are?' as he in turn grabs her imaginary broomstick and shows her that he has had enough (see page 52).

Play-acting **th**.

Act Out Whole Words

The children, as letter people, can ask each other whether or not they will come and 'be' in a certain word. Mr I should refuse, if asked to say his name in the word **try** (tri ..). But he might obligingly 'try', and then show how terribly dizzy this makes him (page 60). This leads him to call on the Yo-yo Man to do the job for him. Sammy Snake, if asked to hiss in the word **place** should refuse, giving the other letters in the word a reason to ask Clever Cat if she will make Sammy's sound for him in the word **place**. She, of course , will accept, but only on condition that the next letter must be a Silent Magic E shooting blue sparks so she can hiss like Sammy (page 120). By these little 'word dramas', the children act out the laws of word structure and you ensure that the fictions have made the phonic facts ineradicable.

Staff on Stage

In schools where the staff is prepared to become the 'goodies' and 'baddies' in a Letterland play, the children seldom forget the occasion. Needless to say the opportunities for reinforcing important teaching points, as well as for providing high-spirited entertainment for all are numerous.

Letterland in Art and Craft Periods

Simple sewing can be based on holes punched in polythene or stiff card. The children sew the path their pencil should take. Two sets of stitches will occur where the pencil would retrace itself.

It only needs paper and glue to make masks or papier maché puppets for all the Letterland animals. Collages of Bouncy Ben and Dippy Duck, which can look very fine on left and right sides of the classroom, will also quietly help any child who may still be prone to reversals. A-Z models, puppets, etc. are easy to make.

Large murals of Letterland can allow children to decide how this mythical land might look. They plan what landmarks and/or objects each character might have around them or make real maps of the place. They can invent alliterative addresses. Older children may like to embark on a Letterland tapestry project to support younger children's learning.

Fireman Fred came first
at fencing and figure skating.

It is also easy to mirror real events such as the Olympics, a royal wedding, an election, etc. The children imagine and create their own version of a similar event in Letterland through artwork, crafts, puppetry, story-telling, etc.

Spell Shop

A Spell Shop for the Wicked Water Witch is an obvious theme. The children write out spells for her shop, (e.g. Mix frogs' toenails, bat wings and beet roots). Naturally they must learn to spell the ingredients for the spells. After all, it would never do to mis-spell a spell!

A Letterland Fete

Holding a Letterland Fete is an easy and educational way to add to school funds. To begin with signs and notices all about the school can be picture coded. Use boxes for irregular parts of words, see page 30. Stalls can become Annie Apple's Toffee Apple Stand, Bouncy Ben's Bakery, Clever Cat's Coconut Shy, etc. A playground corner can become a Ducks' Den (with a D-shaped Duck Door) with disguises inside for dressing up. An Elephants' Entrance and Exit can lead to and from Mr E's Easy Magic show. A display of Fireman Fred's Fire Station can be painted with **f**-words written on foam blobs shooting from his hose, with **fr** words added around **Fr**ed and **fl** words written in many **fl**ames. A Golden Girl's Garden can '**g**row' in a corner, with flowers and **g**reen **g**rapes for sale.

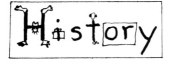

At a more advanced level relay races can be run using **r** and **ar** robber caps instead of batons. Skittles can can be knocked down to resounding **ow** (as in d**ow**n) sounds or **ow** (as in bl**ow**) sounds, depending on which lettered skittles are hit, and so on.

Alliteration leads each school to its own fun, e.g. a Clever Cat's Cook book on sale with recipes contributed beforehand by the mums. As one Head Teacher put it in a letter to parents: 'With your help Letterland Day can be a laughing, loony and learning day, with lots of loot, too!' Her parents were even invited to come dressed as Letterland characters. They did, too, thereby adding considerably to the success of the occasion.

	WITCH AT WORK					air, ear, eer	oar, our, oor	PREFIXES	SUFFIXES		
ir	aw	au	ew	ow	ou	air, ear, eer	oar, our, oor	re pro	ous	ture	tion	ible etc.

Progress Charts

On a more serious note, back in the staff room devote a corner to your Letterland Progress Charts, ideally one for each class to ensure a co-ordinated approach to reading and spelling skills. Then all subject teachers will know which sounds are being taught in any one week. Such mutual support will not only coordinate but accelerate children's progress throughout the school.

tube

volume

electricity

cylinder

Canada

Bahrain

Zaire

coal

fuel

once

twice

weight

height

thirty

thirtieth

Terrington St. Clement Infants, Norfolk.

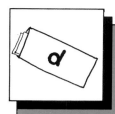

Revision of Single Letter Sounds

For children new to the Letterland characters and children needing revision after the summer holidays the 'Guess the Picture Game' described below can be very useful.

Guess the Picture Game.   This is a popular game with high auditory input and output. Yet it does not appear to be repetitious. Cut out a set of 26 pictures (taken from magazines or from an old alphabet book) one beginning with each letter of the alphabet. Each picture must be different from the Pictogram picture for that letter. For example, the first pictures might show an **a**nt, a **b**oat, a **c**amera, a **d**ragon, and **e**lf, etc. Mount them on the same size and thickness of card as the Picture Code Cards, but show no letter on them.

Each mounted picture should be paired with its Picture Code Card. Place both in an envelope with the plain letter clearly marked on the outside (front and back) of the envelope. The players sit opposite you in a row. The game can be played with only a few envelopes containing pairs, or as many as space will allow. (A blanket spread out on the floor makes a good surface if a large number of cards are going to be used.)

Hold up the envelope marked, for example, with **d** and ask "**d**, for **d**uck, or **d**.. for **d**ragon?" The answer must be not just "the **d**ragon" or "the **d**uck" but "**d**.. for **d**ragon" "or" "**d**.. for **d**uck". The child pulls out one card (a matter of pure chance), keeps it if correct, and displays it, face up, for everyone to see. If s/he has chosen the wrong one it must go back into the envelope, to be re-played later. Each pair is treated in the same way.

Once one letter in a pair has been won the next time round any child who spots that letter already laid out can guess quickly which picture is left in the envelope. This makes the last stages of the game both swift and exciting. The child who has guessed the most cards correctly is the winner.

As the children become well acquainted with the pairs some can take turns at your role, asking the questions.

This game can be made more personal by using photographs of children throughout the school instead of pictures from magazines. The photographs must be clear enough so that each child can be recognised at a glance. A few letters will not begin any names. Pictures suggested for **qu**, **x**, and **z**: 'qu' for 'question mark', 'kss' for 'exit' (e**ks**it) showing door with EXIT sign over it, and 'z' for '**z**oo'.

Motivate to Punctuate

Children become weary of endless reminders not to leave out full stops and capital letters. You may well become weary too, repeating yourself so often. Perhaps a change in your instruction language will help. Suggest that the children give their Letterland friends a chance to do their trick, to get bigger, or jump higher, etc. The Letterland characters become the motivators.

Take a Deep Breath

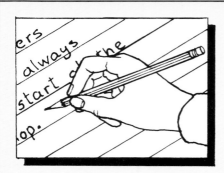

Many of the Letterland characters take a deep breath after a full stop to do their 'get bigger trick' (become capital letters).

Authors of books use full stops together with 'big' capital letter shapes to signal to their readers to stop and take a breath before they read on.

The full stop usually means the end of the last thought. The capital letter signals an important new start. The Letterland characters love starting sentences because they all enjoy feeling important. (Don't we all! Discuss.)

Ask everyone to scan newspapers to find, for example, just sentences 'that open with a Duck Door'. They overwrite the *preceding full stop* and *capital* D in colour. They may go on to look for sentences where 'Poor Peter has popped up', etc. Also point out that to write *any* capital letter, start at the top.

Capitals Wanted

When correcting for omitted capitals you could try talking along these lines. 'If your sentence begins with the [a] sound don't forget to.....'

a A — put your apple on an Applestand.

b B — give Bouncy Ben a chance to do his balancing trick right there at the beginning!

c C — give Clever Cat a chance to do her 'get bigger trick'.

d D — open it with a Duck Door!

e E — give Eddy Elephant a chance to do his 'elephant on-end' trick.

f F — put Fireman Fred up front, all stiff and straight, the way he likes to look when he's doing an important job like starting a name or a sentence.

g G — don't leave Golden Girl in her garden swing when you can give her a go in her Go-Car!

h H — show us how happy you can make the Hat Man by letting him start your sentence with a handstand!

i I –	don't use an ink *bottle*. Use an ink *pen*.
j J –	give Jumping Jim a chance to jump sky high.
k K –	give the king a chance to take a deep breath and kick off this sentence with a nice big kick.
l L –	give Lamp Lady a chance to rest her long, long legs on the line.
m M –	who is going to start it? Munching Mike or his Mum?
n N –	give Naughty Nick a chance to bang in some nails without being called a nuisance, for a change.
o O –	here's your chance to let Oscar Orange take a deep breath and look big and important.
p P –	give Poor Peter a chance to pop up, even though his floppy ears will still droop.
qu Qu –	let the Quarrelsome Queen start the sentence in her Quiet Room.
r R –	here's your chance to show you know how Robber Red looks when he has stuffed stolen goods under his jumper.
s S –	give Sammy Snake a chance to take a deep breath and suddenly look super-sized!
t T –	give Ticking Tom a chance to do his 'get bigger trick' so he ends up with his head in the clouds.
u U –	give Uppy Umbrella a chance to do her 'get bigger trick'.
v V –	here's your chance to decorate the beginning of your sentence with a *very* big Vase of Violets.
w W –	give the Witch a chance to do her 'get bigger trick'.
x X –	let Max have a chance to give Maxine a big kiss.
y Y –	give the Yo-yo Man a chance to step up on to the line to begin your sentence.
z Z –	give Zig Zag Zebra a chance to do her 'get bigger trick'. Maybe then she won't feel quite so shy.

Capital Letters Not Wanted

Conversely, to cure bad habits (e.g. a**B**out or rea**D**y) your wording can be 'No tricks in the middle, please!' Explain that the only time capitals will occur inside words is when *all* the Letterland characters are helping to show how important that word is, e.g. DANGER, book titles, etc.

EXIT

LOOK RIGHT

DANGER KEEP OUT

The All Important Vowels

The exercise which follows has already been set out in 'First Steps'. It is worth repeating, if only for those who are new to Letterland. Hand out 18 of the 21 consonant Picture Code Cards. (Exclude **r**, **w** and **y** at this stage.) Ask what three-letter words the children can make, with all these cards to choose from. The answer will quickly emerge, not a single pronounceable word, because ...? They have no vowels! Every English word must contain at least one vowel. This is also a good time to introduce the word 'consonant' and its meaning.

The consonants are really just lip, tongue and teeth positions. They are useless without the sounds made by the vowels. 'Consonant' means 'with sound'. That is why the consonants in their hands are useless right now! Hand out the *short* vowel cards so that groups of children can make at least 5 real words. Emphasise how busy these vowels must be since no word can be made without at least one of them.

Revision of Vowel Sounds and Vowel Names

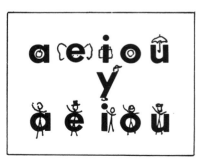

'First Steps' presented the long vowel sounds as 'Vowel Men' and the short vowel sounds as their 'belongings'.

The children met the Vowel Men in a few high-usage words e.g. **say**, **name**, **make**, **play**, **he**, **she**, **me**, **I**, **like**, **no**, **go**, **so**, **use**, **you** and learnt to picture code them with stick men. Apart from these high usage words the focus was on short vowel words. The children should now be confident in facing all new short vowel words in reading and spelling, and at least these 14 long vowel words.

The Vowel Chart For those who need 'topping up' and any new children not yet initiated into Letterland lore, a top priority will be the **a**, **e**, **i**, **o**, **u** and **y** Vowel Scene.

Display this coloured chart for frequent general reference. Have each child also draw their own version of it, no matter how unskilled. This will be a useful activity. They should work *from memory* rather than copying, so as to really make the organisation of vowels on this chart their own.

Vowel Men and their Belongings The essence of Letterland is prediction and most of the sections of this Guide are directed towards this critical skill. Once young readers have learnt the distinction between short and long vowels in any word – in effect, to judge the sound value of a vowel – they are well on their way.

Start by familiarising them with the Letterland distinction between the Vowel Men and their 'belongings'. Ask them to draw Eddy Elephant balancing an **a**pple, an **i**nk bottle and an **o**range on his head and holding an **u**mbrella in his trunk. This is a form of visual shorthand for short vowels. The act of drawing it will 'cluster' the short vowels in the children's mind.

The next step is practice in picture coding short vowel words. The following lists offer convenient examples. With this diet of short vowels well digested, it is then possible to move on to *predicting* when 'a Vowel Man will appear in a word and say his name' (i.e. long vowel). Major strategies for predicting long vowels are successively set out in the sections on Magic **e**, Elephant Endings, Magic **ing** and Vowels Out Walking. Other strategies include Cand**le** Magic and the **'Tion** story. In between are 'sprinkled' strategies for predicting other vowel sounds which are neither long nor short.

(ă, b/d/p)		(ŏ,ĭ, b/d/p/g)		(ă,ŏ,ĭ, d/p/g/)		(ăĕĭŏŭ, b/d/p/g)	
bad	rag	pop	box	rat	pad	at	bag
fat	cap	hit	tin	top	pot	pet	beg
ant	mad	big	hot	sad	fit	did	bog
b p d	b p d	p g d	b g p	dog	flat	dig	bug
p d b	d d p	g d b	p d b	map	stop	disk	dip

(Words including sh, wh and ing)

clocks	jobs	clocks	tell	whisk	drift
lending	tempt	lending	when	bang	slip
hand	bend	hand	rush	bugs	tell
whizz	dust			fuss	when
split	sting			ash	rush

Short-Vowel Phrases

stand back	black socks	flash in the pan	dripping jacket
run up	six lemons	big plums	red ants
thick sticks	damp dog	eleven dresses	logs and rocks
seven pets	pick it up	quick hit	hunt and foxes
lost box	strong legs	wet picnic	splash him

inspect the ticket	silk and velvet	soft drinks
sudden visit	fixing the pockets	lemons and melons
travel by buses	splendid jacket	hitting the jackpot
public events	until it is tested	endless buckets
across the traffic	swiftest rabbit	dentist's address

astonishing	helplessness	fantastic run	selfishness
long telegram	vanishing tracks	magnetic box	limited spending

Box any vowel which is not making its usual sound. (See 'Boxes' page 30).

1. Tim fell and spilt his milk.
2. Helen's dog is licking her hand.
3. Jack was back in a flash.
4. Come and have a drink.
5. Did Bob run to the next bus stop?
6. Dad did not want any apples.

Vowel Men's Habits

In major sections to come (on Magic **e**, Magic Endings and Vowels Out Walking) the emphasis will be on signals *built into words* which tell any uncertain reader when a single vowel will be long. Before that stage it is well for the children to be familiar with the stick man picture coding and to have learnt to 'hear' the Vowel Man say his name as they pronounce any long vowel syllables. In this section the children first focus on a few key words where there is *no* signal. They just learn that the Vowel Men have a habit of appearing regularly in these particular words and saying their names. It is worth having each child draw and picture code important signs. Also they write out and picture code the 'Little Words', 'Kind Words' and 'Old Words' so as to have their own record of them.

The Vowel Men Have a Habit of Saying Their Names on These Signs.

Mr A says his name in D**a**nger.

Mr E says his name in B**e**ware.

Mr I says his name in Pr**i**vate.

Mr O says his name in N**o**tice.

Mr U says his name in M**u**sic.

Vowel Men In Little Words

The Vowel Men have a habit of saying their names at the end of very small words.

a

he   we   go

she be   I   no   you

the   me   hi   so

Kind Words

Mr I has a habit of saying his name in 'Kind Words' because he is such a **ki**nd man. (Add further examples that rhyme with **kind** later, as appropriate: bind, blind, mankind, etc.)

find   kind remind

behind   mind wind

Old Words

Mr O has a habit of saying his name in "Old Words" because he is such an old man. (Add further examples later, blindfold, household, etc.)

old

cold   hold   sold

fold   gold   told

Oscar's Bothersome Little Brother

Over 130 relatively common words, or roughly 1 in every 23 of the 3000 most used words in the language, contain the irregular **o**, pronounced **u** as in **umbrella**.

The historical reason for this irregular sounding **o** goes back to the days when most records were kept by monks and scribes using italic hand-writing. They found that a word like *among* became virtually unreadable unless they broke the pattern of looping strokes. So they closed one of them. The resulting **o** (am**o**ng) is therefore known as the scribal **o**. It is most commonly found beside **m**, **n**, **r** and **v**.

This historical fact cannot be expected to entice younger children, however, to come to grips with the reading problems and spelling frustrations caused by the scribal **o**. Yet the early mastery of this irregularity, at least in high-usage words, is important. Hence Oscar Orange's little br**o**ther.

This bothers**o**me but l**o**vable little fellow was introduced in 'First Steps', but very briefly. Use him now to motivate the children to spot his sound in many more words than are listed below.

Oscar's Bothersome Little Brother Can't Say 'Ŏ'

The youngest of all the Letterland people is Oscar Orange's Little Br**o**ther. He *should* make the same **ŏ** sound in words as Oscar Orange, but he can't. He is too little. Every time Oscar's Little Br**o**ther opens his mouth to say '**ŏ**', out c**o**mes a little '**ŭ**' sound instead! This is why Oscar Orange often calls him his 'Bothers**o**me Little Br**o**ther'. He knows no **o**ther sound! Yet he l**o**ves turning up in words. If only s**o**meb**o**dy could teach him to speak properly. Oscar has tried and so has his m**o**ther. Never mind. They l**o**ve him all the same.

Oscar's brother just comes and says 'ŏ'!

above	coming	front	loving	none	somebody
among	company	glove	Monday	nothing	son
another	cotton	honey	money	other	ton
become	cover	London	monkey	others	won
brother	does	love	month	second	wonder
come	done	lovely	mother	some	wonderful

bothersome

Monday

Old Mr

Picture Coding Contrast Usually the most efficient picture coding for the regular **o** as in **o**range is a filled in orange circle. Oscar can, however, sprout legs to add contrast where his baby brother is also being picture coded. The original coding for long o, the stick man *right through* the letter still stands.

> Picture code
> each o

1. Some mothers have bothersome sons.
2. On Monday my big brother is coming home.

son

Shared Sounds

In Letterland, double consonants are described as 'Shared Sounds' to show that they are both of equal importance. (If you leave one out, it's a mistake!) You will find the Shared Sounds on four double letter cards (**ff, ll, ss** and **rr**) and on eight pairs of single letter cards (**bb, dd, gg, mm, nn, pp, tt** and **zz**). The second card in some pairs (**b**, **d**, **m**, **p** and **z**) is almost identical to the first. (Spot the differences: eyelashes or mouth details.)

Very few common words contain two hard **c**'s as any word search will quickly show.*
At this juncture your focus is simply on two consonants making one simultaneous sound. Later, in 'Best Friend to the Rescue' you will be explaining a vital role often played by the second letter: the chief reason, in spelling, for doubling the consonant.

The children can wear headbands, hold a double

letter card between them (e.g. **ff**), or each hold a matching single letter card (e.g. **b** + **b**) as they play-act the concept of two letters sharing one sound.

Because the **ff, ll, ss** and **rr** pairs are usually permanent features in words their pictograms show both letters on one card. The other letters are provided on single-size cards so that later children can learn by *doing*. They themselves physically add the 'Best Friend' before a Magic Ending. (See page 82 - 85.)

Word Search for Shared Sounds

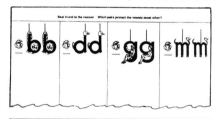
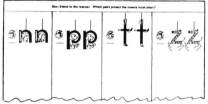

Before you bring out the two double letter Display Charts and remind the children of their **ff, ll** and **ss** Picture Code Cards, you may like to send everyone on a word search to discover for themselves exactly *which* letters frequently share their sounds in words. (Caution: read all of this section before you begin.)

The examples should come from a search of classroom books, but *not* from dictionaries which contain too many currently irrelevant words.

This search is a useful scanning exercise. It encourages rapid eye movement and fosters an information-gathering mental set. Suggest making 'guesstimates'. Which pairs turn up most frequently? Bring out the Display Charts to record findings. Introduce double consonants (best friends) as follows.

Find Some Best Friends in Words

nnnnn...

Everybody likes to have friends. It feels good, too, to be a friend. Most of the people and animals in Letterland are very good friends – without having a particular best friend.

But some have a very best friend. You can easily spot Letterland Best Friends in words because their letters look exactly alike, and they always share their sounds as they appear side by side.

Penny has 2 fuzzy kittens.

---

* No **cc** card is supplied because most common **cc** words contain one hard and one soft **c**. See page 121.

Have everyone scan to see how many Best Friend pairs they can find. This search will bring in examples of many different structures. Accept them all gladly for your 'guesstimate' lists to see which consonant pair wins.

Take Care Before the search begins exclude the vowel pairs **ee** and **oo**. Explain that you *never* find two **e**lephants sharing one sound in a word because **e**lephants are too big to squeeze in side by side! Instead **ee** will be Mr E and his brother 'out walking' in a word. Show the **ee** Picture Code Card and promise a story later (see page 92).

Anyone who spots **oo** will have discovered the mischievous Boot and Foot Twins who do *not* share one sound (nor their boots!). Show the **oo** Picture Code Card and again promise a story later. Other double vowels, e.g. vac**uu**m or sk**ii**ng, are extremely rare. (Put them aside as 'finds' to be treasured.)

Accept words with **cc** but put them aside if the second **c** is soft (as in ac**c**ept). These words will be useful later, when the children can study them to discover which adjacent letter(s) signal a soft **c** (see page 120). Words with **rr** will also be useful later as proof that 'Racing Robbers Rarely Rob' (see page 144).

Let the children discover from their own search results that 13 of the 21 consonants double up in some words frequently.

The examples below are restricted to regular, short vowel words with final **ff**, **ll** or **ss**, useful for dictation. In all cases the double consonant is essential to the root word.

Best Friends at the End: ff

One of **F**iremen **F**red and **F**rank's favourite spots in words is at the *end*. For example, **F**ireman **F**red never sets *off* to fight a fire without his best friend and fellow **F**ireman **F**rank. That is why you always see *two* firemen in the word **off**. Both firemen share their '**f**' sound at the end of these 15 short words. (Not many others end in **ff**.)

off	cuff	huff	ruff	sniff
bluff	fluff	muff	scoff	stuff
cliff	gruff	puff	staff	whiff

They set off with a huff and a puff.

Best Friends at the End: ll

At the *end* of *short* words you will usually see two Lamp Ladies. Why? Well, Lucy the Lamp Lady feels a **l**ittle bit **l**onely at the *end* of **l**ittle words. So she calls in her best friend, Lamp Lady Linda for company. They share their sound and **l**ight up **l**ots of **l**ittle words very we**ll**.

bell	dull	gull	lull	quell	shell	resell
bill	fell	hill	mill	sell	smell	tell
dell	fill	hull	pill	sill	swell	well
doll	frills	kill	quill	shall	still	will

Both Lamp Ladies can spell quite well.

For a special explanation of **all**, **full** and also **-al** and **-ful** see the Giant All and Giant Full stories on page 99.

Best Friends at the End: ss

s	Sammy Snake
ss	hiss fuss

Sammy Snake's best friend is his sister, Sally Snake. They both love to hiss at exactly the same time at the *ends* of short words (especially at the end of the word hi**ss**!).

bless	class	dress	hiss	mess
bliss	chess	fuss	lass	miss
boss	cress	glass	less	press
brass	cross	grass	loss	toss

See also **-less** and **-ness**, page 148.

There are not many hisses they miss.

More Best Friends

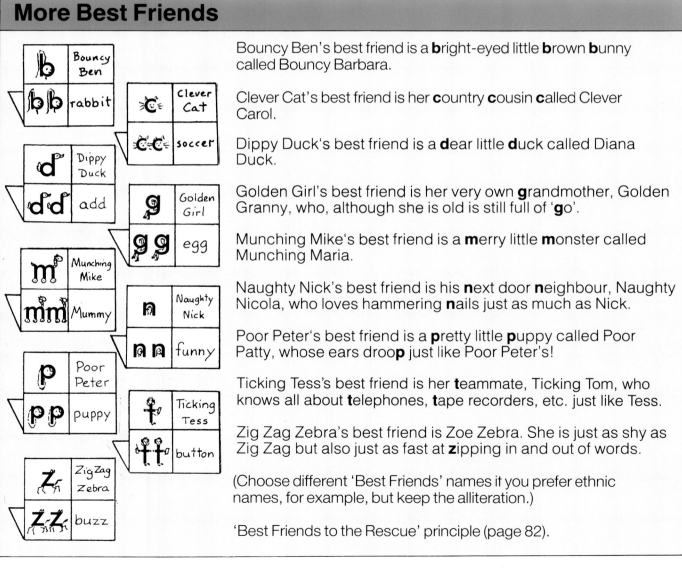

Bouncy Ben's best friend is a **b**right-eyed little **b**rown **b**unny called Bouncy Barbara.

Clever Cat's best friend is her **c**ountry **c**ousin **c**alled Clever Carol.

Dippy Duck's best friend is a **d**ear little **d**uck called Diana Duck.

Golden Girl's best friend is her very own **g**randmother, Golden Granny, who, although she is old is still full of '**go**'.

Munching Mike's best friend is a **m**erry little **m**onster called Munching Maria.

Naughty Nick's best friend is his **n**ext door **n**eighbour, Naughty Nicola, who loves hammering **n**ails just as much as Nick.

Poor Peter's best friend is a **p**retty little **p**uppy called Poor Patty, whose ears droo**p** just like Poor Peter's!

Ticking Tess's best friend is her **t**eammate, Ticking Tom, who knows all about **t**elephones, **t**ape recorders, etc. just like Tess.

Zig Zag Zebra's best friend is Zoe Zebra. She is just as shy as Zig Zag but also just as fast at **z**ipping in and out of words.

(Choose different 'Best Friends' names if you prefer ethnic names, for example, but keep the alliteration.)

'Best Friends to the Rescue' principle (page 82).

The Picture Code Cards for all of the Shared Sounds are supplied with Programme One but are also recommended for use with 'Big Strides', so that both you and the children can set out any word you need in full.

The Hat Man Gets Angry

The stories and pictograms for **sh** and the first sound of **wh** are given in full in 'First Steps'. In brief: the Hat Man always hu**sh**es up Sammy when his pet snake hisses next to him because the Hat Man hates noise. When the Hat Man gets in the Witch's way so that she can't see ahead in the Reading Direction she **wh**acks his hat off, leaving the Hat Man too startled to speak. The second pictogram for **wh**, provided here, explains the few exceptions where the Hat Man gets angry and whacks back. Use the word lists below, first to revise how to code **sh** and **wh**, and then to learn the second sound of **wh**, as in **wh**o. Chart display ideas are on pages 21–25.

The Hat Man Hushes Sammy Snake

ship	shelf	fish	crush	Spanish
shop	ash	selfish	crash	British
shot	ashes	shellfish	smash	polish
shock	dash	sunfish	swish	radish
shut	dish	rush	finish	shrink

Hush, Sammy, hush!

The Wicked Witch Whacks Off the Hairy Hat Man's Hat

white	wheat	whiskers	whiz
while	whim	whack	whirl
whale	whistle	wham	whip
wheel	whisper	whiff	Whitsun

When he's in the way—wham!

She whacks most often in these 5 Question Words:

 when?   which?   why?

what?   where?

The Hat Man Gets Angry With the Witch

After the 5 Question Words (above) the Hat Man has had enough. In the 6th Question Word **who**, he howls at her,

 Who do you think you are!

and whacks off *her* hat. Then it is the Witch who is too startled to speak! (He does it again, too, in **whose, whom** and **whole**.)

See Letterland Songbook and Audio Tape No. 1 for the **sh** and **wh** songs.

Ticking Tom and the Hat Man

The words **the** and **this, that, they, them, there, these, those** and **with** are such high-usage words that they should be sight words long before any child is ready to

learn the two sounds of **th**: the voiced **th** (as in **the**) and voiceless or whispered **th** (as in **th**under). The **th** song in Letterland Songbook and Audio Tape 2B makes a good

starting point for studying the **th** sounds since it relates the **th** story in a quick rhyme. It also requires pronouncing both sounds of **th** several times within the verses.

Tom and the Hat Man Think they Hear Thunder

Like Ticking Tess, Ticking Tom spends most of the time in Letterland sending messages in tiny little ticks like this, 't... t... t...' But have you ever noticed that Tom and the Hat Man make a completely different sound whenever they meet each other in a word? Ticking Tom blames it all on the weather. It is true, there is a lot of wind and rain in Letterland, and thunder storms as well! (Discuss thunder: cause, fear of, etc.)

Ticking Tom is not afraid of the thunder, It's only noise, after all, and noise cannot hurt you. The Hat Man is not afraid either, but do you think he likes it? (Elicit: No!)

Whenever Tom and the Hat Man hear thunder they hate it so much **th**at **th**ey stick out their tongues and say, '**Th**ere's **th**e **th**under!'

Have everyone whisper '**th**under' or practise the whole phrase in a whisper. Ask the children to slide their tongue across their upper front tee**th** as they stick their tongues out, blowing at the same time, and to pay special attention to this movement.

Discussion Point Maybe Ticking Tom *is* a tiny bit afraid of **th**e **th**under. Otherwise why does he always hold on tight to the Hat Man whenever **th**ey **th**ink **th**ey hear **th**under?

> **Picture code each th**

1. There comes a thundering thick cloud.
2. Both of their fathers went with them.

Look out for children who say 'funder' or pronounce **th**ey as 'dey'. (These children will need to be encouraged particularly to stick out their tongues!)

The fact that **th** has two sounds does not need much emphasis at first. When the time is right explain that in some words Tom and the Hat Man are talking (**th**e, **th**em, etc.) while in others they are only whispering (**th**ick, **th**ink, **th**under, etc.) Gradually collect examples on two lists. The class decides which examples go on each one (a difficult but useful exercise in auditory discrimination).

Tom and the Hat Man Speaking Out Loud			Tom and the Hat Man Both Whispering		
the	these	brother	thank	thin	both
this	those	father	think	thinner	with
that	they	mother	thing	thud	moth
them	their	other	thick	thumb	fifth
them	themselves	whether	thicken	thump	sixth
then	thus	weather	thickest	thrush	tenth

Still Whispering: Thursday, Arthur, Beth, Catherine, Dorothy, Jonathan, Judith, Keith, Kenneth, Matthew, Timothy. No thunder (!): Thomas, Anthony, Theresa.

Practise th and f   A suggestion for those who find the **f** and **th** sounds difficult both in their speech and in spelling: when Fireman **F**red puts his **f**ingers to his face and says '**F**ireman **F**red' he can feel his breath on his **f**ingers *twice*. '*You* try saying '**F**ireman Fred' with *your* **f**ingers to your **f**ace. Can you **f**eel your breath **f**lowing out *twice* as you say his name?'

Some Useful Phrases   **F**ellow **F**ireman, **f**ight a **f**ew **f**ires, **f**airly **f**ast, **f**ifteen **f**riends, **f**eel **f**ree, **f**ull of **f**un, Safety **F**irst. Collect and practise them, and others.

Practise th   'When Tom and the Hat Man put **th**eir **th**umbs to their mou**ths** and say '**Th**ere's **th**e **th**under', their tongues wet **th**eir **th**umb **th**ree times. You try wetting your **th**umb **th**ree times as you say '**Th**ere's **th**e **th**under'. If you don't stick out your tongue at least a little bit, watch out, you may be sounding like Dippy Duck or Fireman Fred instead!'

Some Useful Phrases   **Th**ink of a **th**ing, **th**ink of **th**ree **th**ings, **th**ink of **th**ree **th**ousand **th**ings. **Th**anks for **th**e **th**ought. Have you **th**ought it **th**rough? **Th**oroughly **th**ought **th**rough.

Phrases with both f and th   **F**ingers and **th**umb. **Th**in **f**ish. Every**th**ing is **f**ine. **Th**irsty girls **f**irst.

Clever Cat
and the Hat Man

If someone asked you to think of several ways to spell the 'k' sound you would not immediately think of **ch.** Similarly you might not think of **ch** as an alternative for spelling the **sh** sound. Yet

school and **ch**emist are common enough words, and so are names like **Ch**arlotte and Mi**ch**elle. Letterland logic accounts for both the regular and irregular sounds of **ch** with three little stories.

Reserve the second and third ones until they are relevant to reading or to learning to spell a particular word. This section also covers words spelt with **tch** (shown on a separate Flap Chart).

Clever Cat Almost Always Sneezes Beside the Hat Man

Clever Cat belongs to the Hairy Hat Man. He looks after her well and she loves him. But she has one little problem. As soon as she finds herself next to the Hairy Hat Man in a word his **h**airy **h**at makes her nose tickle. So whenever they come together in a word all you can hear is her sneeze, '**ch**. . .'

Can a cat catch a cold?

Explain that cats, like people, find it very difficult to keep their eyes open when they sneeze. So to picture code **ch** draw Clever Cat with her eyes closed and her paw politely raised to cover her sneeze. (To make any child prone to allergies feel in good company you can extend the story. The Hairy Hat Man also sneezes because he is allergic to Clever Cat's fur!)

attach	chicken	enrich	such	chart	starch	cheek
chapel	chill	goldfinch	sandwich	church	torch	each
chat	chimpanzee	inches	spinach	lurch	approach	peach
check	chips	much	which	perch	beach	poach
chess	chisel	ostrich	arch	porch	beech	speech
each	chop	riches	birch	scorch	coach	teach

Charles   Cherry   Rachel   Richard   French   March

Picture code each c and ch

1. Give Carol some chips and a sandwich.
2. The camel had a chat with an ostrich.

Sing and play act the **ch** song in Letterland Songbook No. 2B. Take care that no one sings 'chuh!' You want a *voiceless* '**ch**' sound. Help children to detect the mistake by placing their hands on their throat. If they feel any vibration as they say **ch** they have added voice by mistake.

Clever Cat Does Not Sneeze When the Hat Man's Hat Blows Off

Occasionally the Hat Man's hairy hat blows off. When this happens Clever Cat does not have to sneeze beside the Hat Man because his hat has blown too far away to tickle her nose. Unfortunately for Clever Cat this only happens in a small number of words. When it does, Clever Cat is very pleased to go back to saying "c. . ." for cat. But the Hat Man is too startled to speak, so he says nothing at all.

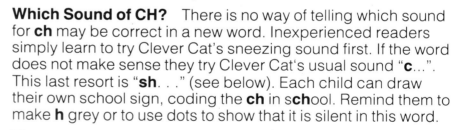

We had chips at the school picnic.

ache	chemist	chrome	headache	scheme	Chloe
aching	chemistry	chronic	mechanic	scholar	Christabel
alchemy	Christmas	chrysalis	monarch	school	Christina
anchor	choir	echo	monarchy	stomach	Christopher
anarchy	chord	epoch	orchid	technical	Michael
architect	chorus	harpsichord	orchestra	technique	Nicholas

> **Picture code both ch sounds**

1. Which children will sing in the choir at Christmas?
2. Did Charles have a stomach ache or was it Richard?

Neither this **ch** Pictogram nor the next one is shown on a Picture Code Card or Flap Chart. When the time is right to explore words such as s**ch**ool and **Ch**ristmas, or words like ma**ch**ine and para**ch**ute (see next story), ask the children to design their own Pictograms. Ideally *describe* but don't *show* them the two Pictograms in this book until after they work out how to draw details to match each story themselves.

Which Sound of CH?   There is no way of telling which sound for **ch** may be correct in a new word. Inexperienced readers simply learn to try Clever Cat's sneezing sound first. If the word does not make sense they try Clever Cat's usual sound "**c**...". This last resort is "**sh**. . ." (see below). Each child can draw their own school sign, coding the **ch** in s**ch**ool. Remind them to make **h** grey or to use dots to show that it is silent in this word.

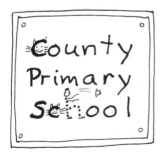

The next Pictogram has low priority except for children with this French pronunciation of **ch** in their names.

Sometimes the Hat Man Hushes Clever Cat Up

We know that *usually* Clever Cat sneezes very softly beside the Hairy Hat Man. But every once in a while Clever Cat sneezes so loudly that the Hat Man has to turn back and say '**sh**!' to her, exactly as he always does to Sammy Snake. That is why in a few words you will hear a '**sh**' sound when Clever Cat and the Hat Man are together.

Let's give Cheryl some cherries.

champagne	charade	chateau	machine	parachute
chandelier	chassis	chiffon	moustache	schedule

> **Picture code each ch**

1. Can Michelle do a parachute jump?
2. Let's play charades with Charlie and Cheryl.

Ticking Tess Says "T..." Very Quietly Beside Clever Cat and the Hat Man

In some words you will see Ticking Tess watching Clever Cat sneeze beside the Hairy Hat Man. Ticking Tess feels sorry for Clever Cat and wishes she could help her. But like the Hat Man, she does not know why Clever Cat sneezes, so Tess just stands there saying "t..." so quietly that no one can hear her at all.

*(Note: Substitute Tom for Tess if your Picture Code Card for **tch** shows Tom.)*

She feels wretched just watching.

Note. Earlier editions of the Picture Code Cards could show Ticking Tom, instead of Tess.

batch	ditch*	hitch	match*	satchel	snatch	twitch
catch*	Dutch	hutch	notch	Scotch	stitches	watch*
clutch	fetch*	itch	patch*	scratch*	stretch	witch*
crutch	hatch*	kitchen*	pitch*	sketch	switch	wretched

* indicates the most useful words in spelling.

> **Picture code each ch and tch**

1. Fetch the fresh batch of buns from the kitchen.
2. The pitch was too wet for the cricket match.

Tch in Spelling Most *one*-syllable words with only one short-sounding vowel just before the 'ch' sound are spelt with -**tch**. Exceptions **much**, **which**, **such** and **rich**.

Follow up: revise sh, ch and tch together Have the children make up phrases and sentences containing both **sh** and **ch**, then picture code them to show Clever Cat, Sammy Snake and the Hat Man's typical behaviour in them.

fish and chips	such fresh chicken	polishing benches
punch and scratch	swish, bump and crunch	rush in and snatch it
flashes from torches	Catch shellfish	pinching and pushing
Did the witch vanish?	kitchen brush	finish lunch
He thinks I am childish.	French or British	Dutch and Scottish

Bunch of radishes.

More About The Hat Man

For reasons best known to children, the Hairy Hat Man is apt to become their favourite, a quiet sort of **h**ero to their mind. He is **h**andsome (in a **h**airy sort of way). He is helpful and good **h**earted. He likes making his pets feel **h**appy, and people too. Each of the following three stories for **ph, gh** and **igh** tells how the letters concerned show consideration towards each other. Teach each story when it best suits your children's needs.

Poor Peter and the Hat Man Say "ph . . . " as in Photograph

The Hairy Hat Man knows Poor Peter is unhappy because his ears droop. He knows also that Poor Peter loves having his **ph**otogra**ph** taken. So whenever he is next to Poor Peter in a word he turns and takes Peter's **ph**otogra**ph** to cheer him up. That makes Poor Peter smile and the Hat Man even laughs; quietly mind you, with his mouth half shut and his teeth on his lips. So his usual '**hhh**' sound becomes a '**fff**' sound just like Fireman Fred. You can hear it twice in the word **ph**otogra**ph**! This is very handy for Fireman Fred when he has to be away fighting fires, because he knows that Hat Man will enjoy taking more **ph**otogra**ph**s of Poor Peter, while making the '**fff**' sound for Fred. (Photograph on back cover.)

Let's take Poor Peter's photograph.

alphabet	graph	orphan	phantom	phone	prophesy	telegraph
elephant	nephew	pamphlet	pheasant	photo	prophet	telephone
apostrophe	decipher	hyphen	phantasy	**ph**otogra**ph**	physical	sphinx
atmosphere	dolphin	nymph	Pharisee	**ph**os**ph**orus	physics	symphony
emphatic	geography	paragraph	phew	phrase	sphere	trophy

Daphne, Joseph, Philip, Philippa, Phoebe, Phyllis, Ralph, Randolph, Rudolph, Sophie, Stephanie.

Picture code each ph

1. Daphne's photo of Philip is by the telephone.
2. The five orphans fed the elephants and dolphins.

Play-act and Sing about ph   Use the Ph Song, Letterland Songbook and Audio Tape 2B to support the story.

Take Photos   If you photograph your own group of children play-acting not only this but also other pictogram stories you will soon have a unique album recording your Letterland work. The children are also likely to enjoy being photographed just as much as Poor Peter!

Golden Girl and the Hairy Hat Man are Silent Together

Golden Girl knows that the Hairy Hat Man hates noise. So every time he stands next to her in a word she keeps completely quiet. So does he. They just enjoy being silent together.

I bought eight buns.

Note. Some Picture Code Cards show Golden Girl (also nicknamed Green Girl) with a long ponytail. Her hair has **grown**!

| although | brought | daughter | ought | thought |
| bought | caught | fought | though | through |

Picture code each gh

1. Has Hugh gone straight home?
2. She caught her cold from her daughter.

Exception: lau**gh**. It seems that both Golden Girl and the Hat Man cannot resist lau**gh**ing softly in the word **laugh**, so **gh** sounds just like **ph**. Also cou**gh**, rou**gh**, tou**gh** and enou**gh**. See 'Over to Them', page 159.

An Ice-Cream for Golden Girl from the Hairy Hat Man

Often when Golden Girl and the Hairy Hat Man are side by side in a word the Hat Man asks Mr I to give Golden Girl an ice cream for being so nice and quiet beside him. In those words Mr I comes right up beside Golden Girl. Then you can hear him saying '**i**' for '**i**ce cream' as he holds out a delicious **i**ce cream for her. That pleases both Golden Girl and the Hat Man very much, so they both smile - silently, of course!

She looks delighted.

| flight | high | highway | hindsight | lightning | sigh | thigh |
| fright | higher | Highness | knight | midnight | sight | tight |

Exceptions No **i** sound before **gh**: eight, straight, weight.

Picture code each igh

1. I like to have a night light on.
2. Her Highness sighed a deep sigh.

Mr Yo-yo Man's Business Deals with Mr I

The letter **y** turns up in a vast number of words. Yet its 'own' sound, as in **y**ellow, only occurs in about 15 of the 3,000 most used words in the language. The Yo-yo Man's few chances to sell yo-yos (make his own sound) occur mainly at the start of words, rarely inside, and virtually never at the end. So the Yo-yo Man has a problem. How can

he make a living just selling yo-yos, not to mention save up for his life's ambition to buy a **y**acht? The answer is the same as in real life: if you cannot work for yourself you work for others. Lead the children to discover where the Yo-yo Man finds other work. Good examples to start with are **yes, try, yellow, my, yet, July**. When they have

registered the long **i** sound in **my**, **try** and **July** the children are ready for the pictogram and story below. This section covers final **y** (as in **my**), medial **y** (as in **rhyme**), medial **y** (as in **rhythm**). For final **y** (as in **very**) see page 102. Allow time between the different stories. For further stories about **y** see **ay**, **oy** and **y–i**.

Why the Yo-yo Man Says "i" for Mr I at the Ends of Words

There are not very many words which need the Yellow Yo yo Man's 'yyy . . .' sound. So the poor fellow has few chances to appear in words and sell his yellow yo-yos. Clearly he could never earn a living from that work alone. Luckily, one day Mr I came rushing up to the Yo-yo Man, calling for help.

"Oh, Yo-yo Man," cried Mr I. "Every time I stand at the *end* of a word to say my name I feel dizzy, as though I were about to fall off a cliff! Could you possibly stand at the end of a few words and say my name for me?"

"Yyyes, I'd be glad to have a go!" the Yo-yo Man replied. Carefully he put down his yo-yo's, took a deep breath and said, "**i**". "That's f**i**ne," said Mr I, full of sm**i**les.

So from that day forward the Yo-yo Man earned more money, working for Mr I at the end of words. He really enjoys the work because Mr I also gives him a great big, free **i**ce cream every time the Yo-yo Man says "**i**" for him.

Mr. I said, "Why not try my job?"

		ply	ally	gratify	rely
my		pry	amplify	imply	reply
cry	Less	sly	apply	justify	satisfy
shy	common	spry	classify	lullaby	signify
sky	words:	spy	defy	magnify	supply
try		sty	deny	multiply	terrify
why					

Picture code each ĭ, ī and y ⟩

1. I'd like to fly in the sky by myself.
2. Try to multiply and then divide it.

Encourage children to overcome habits of misspelling such as **cri**, **ski** for **cry**, **sky** by commenting along these lines: "What? You have put Mr I at the end of a word? Oh, but remember, poor Mr I gets so dizzy at the *end* of a word! Think, whom did he ask in the story to say his name for him? Who needs the work?" The child's correction then becomes almost a rescue act, relieving Mr I from his dizzy position and giving the Yo-yo Man some badly needed work.

To children who write **-iy** you can say, "But surely Mr I would *never* pay the Yo-yo Man to say 'i' for him *and* still stand there saying 'i' himself, would he?" (Not one English word contains **-iy**.)

Exceptions Mr I does put up with his dizzy feeling long enough to say his own name in the little word **hi**. In some words of foreign origin, such as **taxi**, **spaghetti**, **khaki**, **kiwi**, **ski** and **chili** he feels so dizzy at the end that he cries out '**eeee**'! instead of his name 'i'!

Why the Yo-yo Man Says 'i' for Mr I Inside Some Words

Mr I is so pleased that the Yo-yo Man says his name 'i' for him at the *end* of words that he has asked him to help out too by saying his name *inside* a few words. The Yo-yo Man is always glad to have more work. So now the Yo-yo Man regularly says 'i' for Mr I *inside* some words as well as at the end – which earns him more money and more **ice** creams!

I'll buy this type of tyre.

crying	frying	recycling	simplifying				
drying	prying	replying	(and all examples on the previous				
flying	spying	satisfying	list to which **-ing** can be added)				

bypass	dye	dynamite	hydrogen	nylon	scythe	style	typing
cycle	dyed	eye	hyacinth	rhyme	shyness	thyme	tyrant
cypress	dyeing	goodbye	hyphen	rye	skyscraper	type	tyre

Picture code each i and y ⟩

1. The spy was trying to find a stick of dynamite.
2. My eyes sting if I type on that typewriter.

Timing of the Next Y Story The medial **-y-** sound (as in rh**y**thm) has low priority compared with final **y**, which is covered in 'The Business Deal with Mr E', page 102. Wait until a relevant word, e.g. c**y**linder, p**y**ramid or perhaps synon**y**m becomes topical, before telling this last medial **-y-** story.

Why the Yo-yo Man Sometimes Says "i" for Ink in Words

When the Yo-yo Man wants to work out how many yo-yos he has sold, or how much money he has saved up while working for Mr I, he needs **i**nk to do his sums. Usually Mr I provides any word that needs an 'i' sound with an **i**nk bottle. But there isn't always an **i**nk bottle handy.

"Why not give *me* some **i**nk?," the Yo-yo Man asked Mr I one day. "Then I can do my sums *and* say 'i' inside words for you!"

"It's a deal!" replied Mr I (in words of one sy̆llable). This is why you will sometimes see the Yo-yo Man carrying a bottle of **i**nk and making an 'ĭ' sound in words.

I left my̆ bicy̆cle by the gy̆m.

bicycle	gymnasium	oxygen	syllable
crystal	hymn	pygmy	symbol
cylinder	mystery	pyjamas	symphony
gym	myth	pyramid	typical

Beryl, Cynthia, Evelyn, Gladys, Lydia, Lynda, Marilyn, Sylvia, Egypt, Syria, Libya, Olympia.

More advanced:

analysis	mysterious	rhythmic	sylvan
chlorophyl	mystical	syllabus	synonym
chrysalis	physical	symmetric	synthetic
crypt	pterodactyl	sympathy	synagogue
lyrics	rhythm	symptom	tyranny

**Picture code
each i and y**

1. Are his nylon pyjamas dry?
2. What type of system was used to build the pyramids?

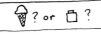

style   myth
cycle   rythm
bicycle   rhyme
Egypt   hyphen
pyramid   gym

Revision   It would be helpful to revise these two sounds of -y-on one sheet at some later stage, listing examples from both stories. The children's 'job' is to decide how to code each -y-.

"Ice cream or ink bottle?", you ask. They learn from this exercise to be flexible in decoding an unknown word with -y- in it. The only decision is: which job is the Yo-yo Man doing for Mr I?

The Boy Called Roy's 'OY' Game

Most children will be able to read the words **boy** and **toys** as sight words long before they need to study the **oy** sound and its two spelling patterns **oy** and **oi** in less common words. Even so they may like to hear the **oy** story early on to reassure them that not only words which they *don't* know but also words they *do* know have story explanations. Later, teach the concept of **y**-changing-to-**i** in the **oi** story. It will tie in with **y**-changing-to-**i**-before-**es**, **ed**, etc. (see page 135). Follow up with the lively **oy** song in Songbook and Audio Tape 2B, with two groups taking the parts of Roy and the Yo-yo Man.

The Boy and the Yoyo Man Play the 'OY' Game at the End of Words

In Naughty Nick's class at school in Letterland there is a b**oy** called R**oy**. At the *end* of words this b**oy** called R**oy** enj**oy**s leap-frogging over an **o** and into the Yo-yo Man's sack. He calls this leap-frog game his '**oy** game' because he likes to shout "**oy**!" as he leaps. The Yo-yo Man shouts "**oy**!" too, every time R**oy** lands on him unexpectedly. The Yo-yo Man pretends to be ann**oy**ed with R**oy**, but really they both enj**oy** R**oy**'s '**oy** game' because they both enj**oy** shouting "**oy**!".

They both enjoy the boy's OY game.

ahoy	buoy	destroy	enjoy	joy	toys
alloy	convoy	deploy	envoy	soy	Joyce
boy	corduroy	employ	gargoyle	tomboy	Troy

Picture code each y and oy >

1. My Dad enjoyed employing the toyshop man.
2. Did the enemy destroy the convoy?

The Boy and the Yoyo Man Play the 'OI' Game Inside Words

Sometimes you will hear the **oy** game being played *inside* a word. Then the game will sound the same but it will not look the same. This is because the Yo-yo Man changes out of his working clothes (which he uses to finish **oy** words), and puts on his neat, straight **i**-clothes because being *inside* words is a tidier type of work. So the '**oy** game' becomes the '**oi** game'. It is really the same game, except that it is a little less n**oi**sy and b**oi**sterous played inside the word.

Roy has a noisy voice.

oy in boy, but **oi** in boil			**oy** in joy, but **oi** in joint	
oy in coy, but **oi** in coin			**oy** in toy, but **oi** in toil and toilet	

adroit	disappointed	join	oil	rejoice
appointment	embroider	jointed	ointment	spoil
boisterous	exploit	moist	pointed	toilet
broil	foil	moisten	poise	turmoil
coil	hoist	noise	poison	turquoise
coin	invoice	noisy	recoil voice	

> **Picture code each y, oy and oi**

1. Joyce has gone and spoiled my pen point.
2. This loin is not a joint for boiling.

Follow Up. Sing the **oy** song again, second verse only.

Exceptions Oy does not change to **oi** when R**oy** and the Yo-yo Man have already been playing the **oy** game at the *end* of a word. Then even if a new ending is added the Yo yo Man does not change. After all he is still finishing up the *main word* – and his game with Roy.

-oys , -oyed , -oying , -oyful , -oyment

enjoy	joy	employ	destroy	boy	coy	annoy
enjoys	joys	employed	destroyer	tomboys	coyly	annoyance
enjoyed	joyful	employing	destroys	boyhood	coyness	annoys
enjoying	joyless	employer	destroyed	boyish	decoys	annoyed
enjoyment	joyous	employment	destroying	boyishness	decoyed	annoying

Also: royal, loyal, oyster.

Sammy Snake and Zig Zag Zebra

When we introduce **s** as a 'hissing' letter we tend to overlook the fact that in 6 out of 10 common words **s** sounds just like **z**. When children hear a **z** sound in large numbers of words perhaps it is not surprising that they are soon reversing both **s**'s and **z**'s! They need to know that **s** and **z** share the **z**-sound and that **z** is rare in spelling. Only four words begin with **z** within the basic 3,000 most used words in the English language. The number of internal **z**'s is also small, whereas a 'hissing' **s** can even switch to a **z** sound within the same word!

(Compare the first **s** in house with both **s**'s in houses.) This section also introduces **s** as a signal meaning plural. **Plural** is a term which you may wish to introduce now. The Plural-Stopper **se** section and the '**s** and **s**' sections which follow can be taught whenever you judge them relevant.

Why Sammy Snake Often Makes Zig Zag Zebra's Sound

Most of the hissing sounds you can hear in words are made by Sammy Snake, who just loves **s**lithering and **s**liding along in words saying, "**sss**!"

But people need Sammy's hissing sound so often in words that he hardly has time to sleep at night. So instead he has lots of quick naps in words. Then his hissing sound turns into a dozing sound.

Often Sammy dozes in words.

This dozing sound, "**zzz** . . ." is just like the "**zzz** . . ." sound made by Zig Zag Zebra.

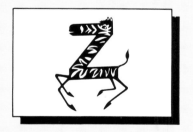

Zig Zag Zips along in words.

Zig Zag Zebra does not mind *starting* a *few* words, but she hates turning up *inside* words because, like all zebras, she is very shy. So she is very glad that Sammy can make the same **zzz** sound that she makes. That way *he* can make most of *her* **zzz** sounds for her in his sleep!

Picture code each s and z

1. These buses come at crazy times.
2. What soft fuzzy kittens!

Picture code each s and s

1. He sent me a present
2. Listen to his soft hisses.

Note: Sammy Snake never falls asleep (never says **zzz**) at the start of a word. You have to be very wide awake to start a word! But he very often doze**s** at the end**s** of word**s**, (see **es** below) wherea**s** Zig Zag only appear**s** at the end**s** of less than a dozen word**s**.

Sammy Snake's Hiss Can Mean "Ssseveral of Sssomething"

When you see Sammy Snake hissing at the end of a word his **hiss** has a special meaning. His hiss means "**sss**everal of **sss**omething".

step, steps ˢˢˢᵉᵛᵉʳᵃˡ   list, lists ˢˢˢᵉᵛᵉʳᵃˡ

Even when Sammy is dozing at the end of a word his hisses *still* mean "several of something". When words end with this "several of something" hiss they are called plural words.

ʂˢˢ Hissing Snake				ʂˣᶻᶻ Dozing Snake			
bats	drinks	maps	sticks	animals	dogs	games	planes
banks	hats	nests	tanks	balls	dolls	girls	schools
cats	hops	picnics	tops	beds	eggs	guns	tables
camps	jumps	pigs	trips	birds	fathers	kings	teachers
desks	insects	rabbits	trucks	cars	friends	miles	times
ducks	lists	rats	visits	days	hills	mothers	years

For **ss** in -**l**ess and -**n**ess, see page 148.

Silent E Can Stop Sammy Snake's Hiss from Meaning "Several of Something".

When a word meaning only "one of something" ends with a hiss, the only way to stop it from looking as though it *must* be a plural word is to add a silent **e** called a Plural Stopper **e**. While this Plural-Stopper **e** does not stop Sammy Snake from hissing, it does stop his hisses from meaning "several of something". (Not on a Picture Code Card or Flap Chart.)

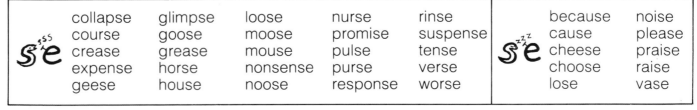

Of course Sammy still makes a noise.

ʂˢˢe	collapse	glimpse	loose	nurse	rinse	ʂᶻᶻe	because	noise
	course	goose	moose	promise	suspense		cause	please
	crease	grease	mouse	pulse	tense		cheese	praise
	expense	horse	nonsense	purse	verse		choose	raise
	geese	house	noose	response	worse		lose	vase

Exceptions: lens, summons.

Eddy Elephant and Sammy Finish some Plural Words Together

When you see Eddy Elephant and Sammy Snake together in Plural Words more often than not Sammy will be dozing, because this is one of his favourite spots for a quick nap.

Good wishes from Sam.

buses	bunches	matches	ashes	changes	badges
buzzes	churches	sketches	fishes	hinges	bridges
horses	lunches	stitches	radishes	oranges	edges
kisses	riches	witches	wishes	sponges	smudges

Often the quick pronunciation of this short **-e** sounds like short **i** instead. To children who write **-is** by mistake, explain that very few words (that *they* will need) end in **-is** and none of them means "several of something". So if in doubt, choose **-es**, not **-is**.

Magic e before s When the **e** before **s** is a Magic **e** it will be silent and should be picture coded as such. Only draw an **e**lephant to illustrate an **ĕ** *sound* (see also Magic **est,** page 76).

The Belonging-Peg Comma

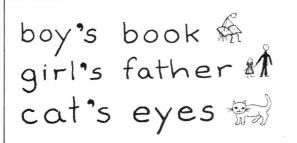

When you see a comma hanging over a word it may be a 'belonging-peg' comma. This comma shows that something belongs to the word in which the comma appears.

When you want to show belonging, how can you decide which side of Sammy to place your comma?

Place the comma behind Sammy's back for *Belonging*

If you want the word to signal "belonging to" put the belonging-peg comma behind Sammy Snake's back.

Place it in front of Sammy's nose for Plural *Plus Belonging*

To signal both "several of something" and "belonging to" let Sammy say "ssseveral" first. Then add your 'belonging-peg' comma.

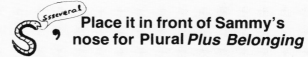

Mr E's Special Invention: Silent Magic e

If you can teach children how to **predict** the correct pronunciation of the vowels you will have spared them much frustration in learning to read. Learning to spot final **e**'s is an important predictive strategy. Many children can parrot the rule Silent **e** makes the vowel before it say its name, but when they meet an unknown silent **e** word they fail to apply the principle. Use the Magic **e** story to ensure that your children do! Not only are there a great many Magic **e** words but Magic **e** is the *first* of a series of Magic Endings which will enable the children to predict the presence of long vowels in a vast number of *other* words as well (see the sections on **ed**, **en**, **est,** and **ing** for a start.) The time you spend play-acting the function of Silent Magic **e** will be worth every minute it takes.

Later a real grasp of the 'Magic' principle will enable young spellers to predict when to double the consonant in thousands of words. This can save literally years of spelling mistakes.

The Vowel Sounds and the Vowel Men

Begin by referring to your coloured Vowel Scene. The odds are that any *single* vowel will make a top row sound, unless the children can spot a signal to indicate that one of the Vowel Men (in the bottom row) will be appearing in the word. The trick is for the children to learn to run their eyes along to the *end* of the word in order to spot the signal. (Remember, Magic **e** is just the *first* signal for them to learn to look out for.)

The Picture Code Card for this final **e** in 'First Steps' is *grey*, just to show that it is a silent letter. 'Big Strides' provides a hollow Magic **e** Picture Code Card for you to colour red – the 'stop, look and listen' colour – to emphasize this silent letter's power as a predictive signal. The **y** appears on this chart as well because (as one 8-year old put it) "he is a part-time vowel".

Display the 'Naming Game' Scene as you tell the following story. This will ensure that everyone remains clear as to 'who' the Vowel Men are while you speak about them.

Why Mr E Invented a Silent Magic E

The Vowel Men work so hard behind the scenes, putting **a**pples and **o**ranges and **i**nk bottles and **u**mbrellas into words, that they seldom have the fun of appearing themselves in words. One day Mr E decided that this would not do. His friends, the Vowel Men, should have a chance to be in words more often. But how could he bring this about? He had to think up a new magic trick! Off he went to work on a very special new kind of **e**. When it was ready he called Mr A, Mr I, Mr O and Mr U together and with a flourish he announced his new invention.

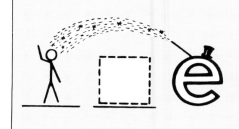

"Introducing the **e**
you cannot hear,
with power to make
Vowel Men appear!"

The brand new **e** was bright red and it had a top hat and a wand, just like Mr E himself. "Imagine," Mr E went on, "that Mr A has just put **an a**ppetizing **a**pple into the word t**a**p."

(Write **tap** very large on the board or, better still, use an overhead projector with **tap** written beforehand in large permanent black letters. Draw a bright red apple inside **a**.)

"Now everyone can see the **a**pple's sound in **tap**. Right? Then I come along with one of my new Silent Magic **e**'s and put it carefully at the end of the word. Now comes the magic moment. A shower of sparks shoot back on to the **a**pple. Hey presto! The **a**pple disappears, and Mr A appears in its place. Mr A waves his arm and shouts his name, proving that my Magic **e** really works. I think we might call it the 'Naming Game'!"

Discuss what it would be like if we could make our friends appear as easily as Mr E manages to, just by shooting Magic Sparks from the end of a word!

Show how the Naming Game also gives the Vowel Men a chance to make new words. By saying his name Mr A has changed **tap** into a brand new word, **tape**!

Point out that if *we* add one of Mr E's Silent Magic **e**'s to the end of a word *we* can make Mr A appear, too, to make a new word.

Try **mad/made** and **plan/plane** together on the board. Add the coding yourself in contrasting chalk before pronouncing the new words together.

Play-act tap/tape Have a picture of a tap and a real tape measure handy to emphasize how 'Magic' can transform a word's *meaning* as well as its *sound*. When the **a**pple child vanishes make sure that the Mr A child throws up his right arm, as pictured on the Naming Game Flap Chart.

Use two children for Mr E and the Magic **e**. From the far right Mr E sends the Magic **e** child to the end of the word to shoot the Magic Sparks. (Remember Mr E himself is the symbol for **long e**, as in **he**.) The Magic **e** child should *not* wear a top hat. Instead the top hat should be drawn on the Magic **e** which he or she is holding. Yellow crepe paper strips on a rod makes a very effective wand. (See page 40.)

Write the words **The Naming Game** boldly above the Chart, with space to add examples as they become appropriate. Have the children watch as you picture code the word **Game**. (Later, when you study Magic **ing**, add the coding for the word **Naming**, see page 80.)

If you happen to have a **Jane**, **James** or **Kate** in your class you can now congratulate them on having Magic **e**'s in their names. Take care though, as names include all too many exceptions, e.g. Carol**ine** but Cather**ine** and Christ**ine**. (The last two **e**'s have suffered 'power failures'! See page 74.)

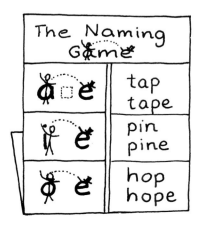

As you introduce words where the other Vowel Men say their names gradually add the examples on the left beside your Magic **e** Flap Chart.

The words listed below are particularly useful because they are meaningful with and without a final **e**.

at	cap	fad	gap	hat	mad	mat
ate	cape	fade	gape	hate	made	mate
pan	plan	rat	Sam	scrap	tap	van
pane	plane	rate	same	scrape	tape	vane
bit	fin	kit	quit	rid	rip	shin
bite	fine	kite	quite	ride	ripe	shine
slid	slim	spin	Tim	trip	strip	win
slide	slime	spine	time	tripe	stripe	wine
glob	hop	mop	not	rob	slop	
globe	hope	mope	note	robe	slope	
cub	cut	plum	tub	us	human	
cube	cute	plume	tube	use	humane	

plan
plane

Use Picture Coding When you ask the children to draw the sparks firing back from the Magic **e** you are asking their hands to do what their eyes and minds must do: to take into account a word <u>ending</u> and its effect on the <u>preceding</u> vowel. They *must* draw their sparks from right to left (not left to right) and *back* over ONE letter, to land on the vowel.

Use the Magic E Song Have some children softly chant the verses below while three or four others take turns on the blackboard. They use red chalk to add a Magic **e** to each short vowel word, and yellow chalk to add the sparks and a stick man through the preceding vowel. (Music on Letterland Songbook and Audio Tape 2B.)

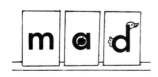

Draw your wand	
Shoot every spark	(Draw wand)
Jump back one letter	
To land on the mark.	(Add sparks)
It's always the same.	(Add stick
The Vowel Man says his name.	figure of
Whenever Magic lands on him	vowel man
The Vowel Man says his name.	through vowel)

Use the Picture Code Cards Set out a short vowel word on a chalkboard ledge for a child to add a Magic **e**, draw the sparks and cover the **a**pple card with the new Vowel Man card. Reverse the procedure too, so that the children make words like **mad, made** and again **mad**. Have them describe to you in their own words what they have just done. Ask "What kind of a game is the Vowel Man playing, when Magic makes him appear in a word?" Elicit "The Naming Game!"

Make 3-D Words Hand out all 'First Steps' consonant cards plus the 5 short vowels, and 5 long vowel cards. Add the 5 'Big Stride' vowel cards, including Magic **e** (with the power-cut **e** on the reverse). You call out words. The children decide whether they are holding a relevant card to be in that word. Appoint one or two children to help in sequencing.

Take Care If you demonstrate the arched path of the magic sparks while facing the children, make sure to reverse the direction of your arm and hand gesture. Alternatively, always turn your back to the pupils while demonstrating the path of the sparks, so that the Reading Direction is the same for you both.

Scour the Environment Spot Magic **e** everywhere. Shop signs often include words like **price, size, shade, sale**. Road signs and the children's own addresses will often include **Lane, Drive, Gate, Close, Grove, Place, -dale**. Household items will include **volume, tone, long wave, flakes**. Empty boxes, packets, wrappers, sweets, etc. will contain some Magic **e** words. Have the children search everywhere!

Newspaper headlines are another source for Magic **e** words, with a range not likely to occur in children's books. So they can take special pride in working out more adult words like

BLAME	EXILE	ESCAPE	CRIME	PROBE
RATE	SCOPE	PROMOTE	CASE	DEBATE
ESTATE	POPE	REFUSE	STOCKPILE	DECLINE

The children might even enjoy constructing their own Magic **e** headlines for their classmates to read:

RISE IN VOLUME OF TRADE   **BRIDE ELOPES**

ATHLETES COMPETE FOR PRIZE   **CLOSE SHAVE**

DISPUTE BRINGS STRIKE   **VOTE STALEMATE**

NEW SCHEME   **FOREST BLAZE**   **BRIDGE UNSAFE**

It can be useful – and quick – to construct words by partly writing them by hand. Use the cards just to highlight important areas.

Instruction Words   Many instruction words are also Magic **e** words – another very good reason for children to understand the Magic **e** principle.

writĕ tracĕ usĕ takĕ describĕ
relatĕ definĕ underlinĕ namĕ
statĕ includĕ substitutĕ
completĕ replacĕ closĕ makĕ
dividĕ reducĕ

(On fire extinguisher)   (On train door)
STRIKĔ KNOB   SLIDĔ TO OPĔN

> **Picture code each vowel**

1. I plan to take the five o'clock plane.
2. Can he take this cane home with him?
3. Sam made the same mistake that time.
4. We made up a mad, home-made game.

I plan to takĕ the fivĕ o'clock planĕ.

Enjoy the Mistakes   If you present Magic **e** mistakes with humour everyone can enjoy them. Do this by pronouncing each mistake exactly as the symbols dictate. Marvellous pieces of nonsense can result. The Magic **e** omitted from a **tube of toothpaste** leaves the child with a **tub of toothpaste**! Omitted from **pine logs** leaves **pin logs**; a **huge gate** becomes a **hug gate**; **scrape those boots** becomes **scrap those boots**. Children who spell **like** as "lick" find themselves licking all sorts of unlikely (or unlicky) things. A **secret code** becomes a **secret cod**. Some children appear to like catching **plans** instead of **planes. I hate you** becomes **I hat you**! A quaint effect is produced by pronouncing **mistake** as "mistak" etc. Odd questions can arise, like "How hot is **sunshin**?", "Can that jet fly around the **glob**?"

Conversely, a child who adds a silent **e** for good measure where it doesn't fit, can be jokingly chided for his unintended results, for example: "I will **wine** that race", "Get **ride** of it quickly", "my fishing **rode** is bent", "the boys are **glade** they came". Ask the child how this word must be pronounced, given his particular spelling. Then have a good laugh over it. The point will ride home on the laughter.

Magic e Word Lists   The number of these lists shows the importance of the Magic **e** principle, operating as it does in more words than it is feasible to count. A complete list would take many pages.

ă – ĕ

ace	blame	date	gave	make	sake	stale
ale	blaze	daze	grace	male	sale	stake
ape	brake	escape	grade	mane	sane	state
age	brave	fake	grape	name	scale	take
amaze	cake	fame	grave	page	shake	tale
awake	came	flame	haze	pale	skate	tame
bake	cane	frame	jade	place	slave	trade
base	case	gale	lame	plate	space	unsafe
behave	cave	game	lane	race	spade	wake
blade	crate	gate	late	safe	spate	wave

admire	describe	hire	line	pride	slice	time
advise	divide	ice	mice	prize	slide	twice
alive	drive	inside	mile	quite	smile	vine
arise	file	invite	mine	rice	spite	while
arrive	fire	invite	mine	rise	strike	white
beside	five	life	nine	side	stripe	wide
bike	glide	like	pine	size	tide	wire
bride	hide	lime	price	shine	tile	wise

alone	code	drove	hope	phone	smoke	those
awoke	coke	expose	hose	poke	spoke	throne
bone	cone	froze	joke	pole	stole	tone
broke	cope	grope	mole	quote	stone	whole
choke	dose	hole	nose	rope	stroke	woke
close	doze	home	note	rose	suppose	zone

accuse	assume	dispute	fuse	minute	refuse
acute	confuse	excuse	huge	perfume	tune
amuse	consume	fume	mule	reduce	volume

Less pure **u** sound (like **oo**)

brute	flute	June	prune
exclude	include	Luke	rude

complete	eve	extreme	Japanese	these	stampede
concrete	Eve	Irene	Pekinese	scene	Steve

Exciting Magic E Words

How many can you include in one story?

accuse	daze	glide	include	mistake	rise	space
amaze	escape	globe	infiltrate	module	satellite	strike
blockade	excite	grenade	inflate	navigate	save	surprise
capsule	explode	hostile	invade	prize	shine	unsafe
collide	flame	ignite	maze	refuse	smoke	unwise

Telegram: ADVISE STEVE BASE UNSAFE FOR USE

More Magic e Words: More Difficult Vocabulary

accumulate	convene	gratitude	multitude	remote
aggravate	corrode	grave	namesake	renovate
alpine	decade	gravitate	nickname	scene
anecdote	decline	grope	obsolete	schedule
athlete	decorate	humane	oppose	stimulate
attitude	dedicate	immune	paradise	strive
attribute	distribute	impolite	participate	televise
bedtime	drape	incline	polythene	textile
blaspheme	dynamite	institute	pose	theme
blockade	educate	irritate	precede	thrive
brigade	erase	landscape	punctuate	tribute
capsize	expose	latitude	radiate	trombone
cascade	fabricate	longitude	recognize	undertone
cellophane	fascinate	magnitude	refine	vile
chide	female	makeshift	relate	wane

I presume the crocodile is not a polite reptile.

Magic e Before s

athletes

tunes

Watch out for magic **e**'s followed by plural **s**. They are still Magic, even when 'hidden' behind Sammy Snake's back. (See also page 66.)

Picture code every vowel				
flames	dukes	fists	brakes
plans	drakes	poles	bricks
caves	bones	piles	bits
planes	lists	pumps	bites
ducks	pines	tubes	dogs

Power Failures

gone

home

PRIVATE

 As soon as we try to teach the Magic E principle, exceptions seem to turn up everywhere! This is because 21 out of 60 of the most common silent **e** words do not obey the rule. They are: **one, gone, done, come, some, more, before, here, where, there, were, sure, store, care, minute, have, give, love, live, above**. All are among the 200 most used words in the language. Consequently they abound in most books and in children's free writing.

To deal with the exceptions as well as the rule explain that, as with all kinds of power, occasionally Magic **e**'s power runs out. (Most children have experienced power cuts.) A child who notices, for example, that the **o** in **gone** is not saying its name can be congratulated for having discovered a Burnt-Out Magic **e**. They illustrate these **e**'s by drawing a wisp of smoke emerging from the wand to demonstrate the power failure. Start a special collection of them.

one minute engine whose machine lettuce

promise done shone purchase college manage

Can the value of the vowel in Burnt-Out Magic **e** words be predicted? It will keep its original sound (as in **gone**) or it becomes irregular. The irregular ones are particularly difficult for low-visualizers to spell. Each child should make their own private collection of these words.

Words Ending in ve

Since all the **v**ases of **v**iolets (**v**'s) in Letterland have little or no base, the slightest breeze can blow them over! Because the winds in words always blow in the Reading Direction the risk is always that a **v**ase will tip over this way → unless it is propped up by a Vase-prop **e**. Vases are safe from the wind inside words but never safe at the end. (No English word ends in **v**.)

Vase in danger . . .of falling over   Vase safe.

When words end in -**ve** the sound of the previous vowel tends to be unpredictable. The three likelihoods are listed:

Short Vowel		Oscar's Little Brother	Boot Twins With One In Hiding
forgive	active	above	disapprove
give	expensive	dove	disprove
have	(and the many	glove	improve
live	other words	love	move
olive	ending in **tive**		prove
relive			

Occasionally the functions of a Vase-prop **e** and a Magic **e** are combined. Picture coding them is quite illuminating! (This pictogram is on the reverse side of the **ve** Picture Code Card.)

have but behave

live but alive

Picture code each vowel and ve →

date	amuse	hate	above	like
love	have	give	nose	lake
lift	rope	blame	rack	lame
shame	clips	slam	rake	slim
move	glove	nine	lick	stone

Elephant Endings are Magic Too

When a silent Magic **e** ceases to be silent (e.g. inflat**e** but inflat**ĕd**, wid**e** but wid**ĕn**, rip**e** but rip**ĕst**), that **e** is still an important signalling letter. Once it becomes buried within the word, however, how can we keep children alert to its continuing function as a predictive signal? The Letterland answer is to call the whole ending 'a Magic Ending'. The **ed, en, est** endings are the first of a number of Magic Endings to which the children should become alert. Because these three begin with a sounded **e** it is convenient to group them as 'Elephant Endings' and to tell the following story about them.

Mr E's First Elephant Ending: ed

When Mr E first invented his special Silent Magic **e**'s Eddy Elephant was full of **e**nvy. "Can't I learn that trick, too?" he asked. "I want to shoot Magic Sparks as well. I **e**njoy seeing the Vowel Men play the Naming Game."

"What a very good idea!" said Mr E. "Wear my hat and take my wand. But mind, you will need at least one partner for this trick."

Just then, who should come waddling along but Dippy Duck. "Ah, Dippy Duck, would you like to come and help?" called Mr E. "I am putting Eddy Elephant in charge of some Magic Endings from now on, but he will need the help of at least one other letter to end the words with him. How about you?"

"Yes indeed!" replied Dippy Duck, wiggling her tail feathers with delight. "Good!" said Mr E. "First Eddy will go to the end of the word. Then the moment *you* arrive to finish the word Eddy Elephant will let the Magic Sparks fly. Hey presto! An **a**pple (or an **o**range or **i**nk or **u**mbrella) will disappear and a Vowel Man will appear to say his name instead – exactly as with my Silent Magic **e**!"

Mr E decided that Ed could help.

ed			
crate	divide	code	flute
crated	divided	coded	fluted
hate	invite	quote	mute
hated	invited	quoted	muted
trade	side	vote	include
traded	sided	voted	included

fad _ _
stamped _ _
cod _ _
chid _ _
conclud _ _

Can You Handle This Elephant Ending? Have the children write out, in very large letters, these five words – all to end in **ed**. They picture code **ed**, fire back the sparks, add the Vowel Man stick figure and then discover what word they have made. The examples are deliberately less familiar words to show that even unknown words have *predictable* pronunciation once the child has learned that **ed** is a Magic Ending.

*See next page

More Elephant Endings

Eddy Elephant has learned to aim the wand just right, so that the Magic Sparks jump back over exactly *one* letter, make a vowel disappear and make a Vowel Man appear to play the Naming Game – just like Mr E's silent Magic **e**'s. Eddy Elephant gets quite excit**ed** shooting the Magic Sparks! He and Nick have ev**en** learnt to make Mr E himself appear and say his name in one or two words.

even   Steven

Mr E, in turn, is so pleased and proud of his pet elephant that he has put him in charge of a third Elephant Ending: Magic **est**. All three Elephant Endings, Magic **ed**, Magic **en** and Magic **est** give the Vowel Men many more chances to play the Naming Game.

bravest   finest   wisest

woven

en		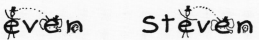 est	
mistake	broke	late	ripe
mistaken	broken	latest	ripest
froze	wide	nice	cute
frozen	widen	nicest	cutest

Double consonants before **-en** and **-est**. See page 82.

How to Choose Between -est and -ist. Use the **est** pictogram not only to teach the **est** suffix as a Magic Ending but also to help to clarify the difference between **est** and -**ist**. We all tend to pronounce -**est** and -**ist** alike, e.g. **hottest** and **artist**. Which spelling to choose? Explain that Magic **est** is used to spell words which mean **the most** (e.g. the most hot, or **hottest**). By comparison **ist** means **one who** (e.g. art**ist**, chem**ist**, dent**ist**, flor**ist**, typ**ist**, pian**ist**, novel**ist**, motor**ist**), so where pronunciation gives no indication, the meaning of the ending may provide the clue.

est = the most

ist = one who

77

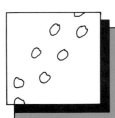
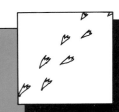

The Three Sounds of - ed

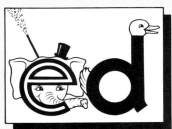

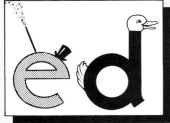
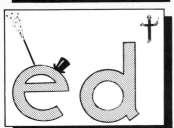

Eddy Elephant and Dippy Duck have found another way to make it exciting to be together in this Magic Ending. Quite often they play a disappearing game! You *may* find them each making their own sound, as expectĕd.

As expected

On the other hand you may find Eddy Elephant has disappeare**d**, leaving not a trace of sound behind him!

Disappeared

Even more amazing, sometimes both Eddy Elephant **and** Dippy Duck have vanished. The only person who ever sees them vanish is Ticking Tom. He is so astonished that all he can say is '**t**' as usual. So the three sounds of this Elephant Ending are **ed, d** and **t**. But have you noticed? Even though the **e**lephant and the **d**uck disappear, the Magic *never* disappears.*

Vanished (t)

Both as expect**ed**		Elephant disappear**ed**		Elephant & duck vanish**ed**	
ended	added	banged	begged	bumped	clipped
handed	batted	buzzed	crammed	clicked	dipped
hunted	dotted	filled	dragged	cracked	dressed
landed	fitted	filmed	drugged	crashed	flopped
lifted	jagged	hinged	robbed	helped	fussed
melted	padded	killed	rubbed	jumped	sniffed
rented	plodded	lived	skinned	milked	snapped
shifted	ragged	longed	tanned	thanked	stuffed
wicked	spotted	smelled	wagged	wished	tripped
completed	aided	blamed	cleaned	based	approached
commuted	coasted	lined	died	choked	coaxed
decided	painted	phoned	failed	coped	increased
faded	pleaded	saved	peeped	priced	peeped
graded	raided	supposed	rained	produced	reached
hated	speeded	surprised	seemed	scraped	released
skated	threaded	tamed	stayed	stroked	soaked
voted	waited	used	tried	used to	screeched
attempted	converted	abandoned	alarmed	attacked	divorced
attracted	departed	belonged	hardened	addressed	immersed
expected	discarded	blackened	performed	developed	remarked
invented	inserted	happened	remarked	discussed	reinforced
visited	reported	summoned	uncurled	embarrassed	reversed

* This means that a single vowel may need protection from Ed's sparks! See 'Rescue' section, p. 82.

1. He jumped and skipped on the ice.
2. I am not used to the equipment which he used.
3. He gripped my hand and patted me on the back.
4. They supposed that we wished to be collected at two.

used

used to

Coding these three different sounds of **ed** is a good exercise in auditory discrimination. Do not be surprised if some children need quite a little help at first. Each word ending in **-ed** should be pronounced aloud naturally, but with a little exaggeration on the final syllable. A whispered **-ed** will always sound like 't'!

Learning the three sounds of **ed** helps children to work back from understandable errors such as **usd, trid, raind, stopt, snapt, helpt, crasht**, etc. Tell them that occasionally **t** will be correct (e.g. **slept, wept**) but the odds are greatly in favour of **-ed**.

invitid ✗

invited ✓

Mistakes Based on -id The **ed** ending is apt to be pronounced 'id', leading to spelling errors such as invit**id**. Tell any child who favours **-id** that the word **did** is almost the only English word which *is* spelt with **-id.** Nearly all the others *must* be spelt with an **-ed**. So even if the ending <u>sounds</u> like **-id** the odds are hugely in favour of **-ed**.

Follow Up Devise an Elephant Dance to perform in assembly, where half the elephants hold in their 'trunks' words written large on cards and the other half hold **ed**/**ed**/**ed** endings. All lumber about but join up with the appropriate words as they swing round to the front, where the audience can read them out loud. Ask the audience to exaggerate their pronunciation of the 3 sounds of **ed** as they read.

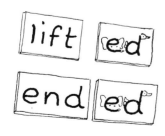

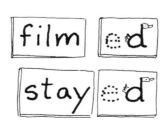

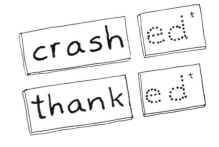

How -ing Became a Magic Ending

The **ng** sound, introduced in 'First Steps' (page 99), explains how Naughty Nick and Golden Girl together make a new si**ng**ing sound whenever they meet in a word. The Bell Ringing Song on Letterland Audio Tape 1 gives practice in the -**ing**, -**ang**, -**ong**, -**ung** sounds.

Further examples are set out below, for revision.
This section then focuses on the signalling power of -**ing**. It is the first Magic Ending that does *not* begin with an **e**, but its power as a predictive signal is exactly the same. In fact there are fewer exceptions than in Magic **e**

words – fewer power failures! So Magic -**ing** is a very reliable signal. As long as a previous *single* vowel is only *one* letter away the sparks will shoot over, make the vowel sound disappear, and make a Vowel Man appear in its place.

Nick and Golden Girl enjoy Singing '-ng'

along	clang	dong	flung	ring	spring
bang	clung	fling	hang	rang	string
cling	ding	fling	long	rung	strong

sing, sang, song, sung

Sometimes Naughty Nick and Golden Girl even sing together twice in the same word!

angry	dangling	jungle	ping-pong	singsong
banging	ding-a-ling	longing	prolonging	strength
belonging	fungus	lungs	ringing	triangle
boomerang	gong	lightning	singing	twang
bungalow	hanger	oblong	slinging	winging
clanging	hangman	orangutang	stinging	wringing

-ING is a Magic Ending

The most exciting thing about the **ing** ending has still to be told. **Ing** is a Magic Ending, just as magic as Magic **e**, Magic **ed**, Magic **en** and Magic **est**!

Why doesn't Magic **ing** begin with **e** like all the other Magic Endings? Actually it happened by chance. One day just after Mr E had invented his Magic **e**'s he took off his top hat and in an absent-minded moment set it down on an **ing** ending. His head must still have been very full of magic because suddenly the **ing** ending started zzz**inging** with magic! Mr E was amazed at first. But then he decided it might be quite excit**ing** to keep **ing** as a Magic End**ing**. So he left a spare wand and top hat right there. Ever since then **ing** has been a Magic Ending! Naughty Nick and Golden Girl find that very excit**ing**.

Using Magic is quite exciting.

Picture-code each vowel and ing.

1. When we went skating he kept smiling and joking.
2. She will be providing us with appetising snacks.

Magic -ing's Sparks   These jump back over one letter exactly the way Magic **e**'s jumping yellow sparks to land on a vowel. Support this point with the song 'Draw Your Wand', Letterland Audio Tape 2B. Its words apply not only to Magic **e** but also to **ing** and *every* other Magic Ending. Stress that the magic sparks can only transform *single* vowels. See also page 68.

take	like	hope	use
tak. .	lik. .	hop. .	us. .
taking	liking	hoping	using
name	drive	joke	include
nam. .	driv. .	jok. .	includ. .
naming	driving	joking	including
escape	collide	explode	presume
escap. .	collid. .	explod. .	presum. .
escaping	colliding	exploding	presuming

Don't Waste Magic

In fact, **ing**'s magic has become very useful because people are always adding **ing** to Magic **e** words. This means they can save the Magic **e** because Magic **ing** can shoot the sparks to play the Naming Game. It is very important to save the Magic **e**'s because in Letterland magic is very precious stuff. It should never be wasted!

Explore the structure of some longer words. Choose deliberately difficult examples to check whether the children can correctly keep a sharp look out for Magic **-ing**. At *every* syllable (except **ing** itself) ask them what they should draw to code the vowels in the first **a** of c**a**scading, "**A**pple or Mr **A**?" and again "**A**pple or Mr **A**?" for the second **a**; similarly "**O**range or Mr **O**?" in c**o**nsoling; "**I**nk or Mr **I**?" in distr**i**buting; "**E**lephant or Mr **E**?"; "**U**mbrella or Mr **U** himself?" etc, as they come to each vowel.

cascading	fabricating	entwining
consoling	distributing	attributing
nominating	convening	gravitating

The children will soon discover that they can read big, difficult words before they even know their meaning; a good demonstration of the value of **ing** as a predictive signal. This strategy is also an important precursor to predicting when to double the consonant (see page 82).

Best Friend to the Rescue Stop the Naming Game!

In this section your aim is to show the most frequent function of double consonants: to protect short vowels. The word *tăp* without a second **p** before Magic **ed** or Magic **ing** will be transformed into **tāped** or **tāping** because there is nothing to stop the Magic Sparks from landing on the short vowel, making a Vowel Man appear in its place. Similarly **hŏp** will become

hōped or **hōping**. Just as they play-acted the Magic **e**'s function in **tăp** and **tāpe**, let the children now act out the wand waving and vowel change caused by Magic **ed** in **tăp**, **tāped** and **hŏp**, **hōped**. Congratulate the Mr A and Mr O children for making these two new words with the help of Magic **ed**. Then present everyone with the problem: what should they do if they don't want **tăp** (or **hŏp**)

to be changed into a completely different word? What if they *want* to write **tăpped** (or **hŏpped**)? Some children may know that two **p**'s are needed. Your aim is to see that not only these children but every child in your care has grasped the second consonant's vital function. The following story is the Letterland answer to the problem.

Stop the Naming Game – But How?

Mr E, the Easy Magic Man, found it very **eee**asy to invent his Magic E's with their beautiful jumping yellow sparks. He also found it very **eee**asy to teach Eddy Elephant to shoot the sparks back over exactly *one* letter in Elephant Endings like **ed** and **en** and **est**. It was **e**easy, too, for him to make Magic Sparks fly from **ing**, once the magician had made **ing** into a Magic Ending as well. So now there were lots of chances for his Vowel Men friends to play the Naming Game, and Mr E was very pleased indeed.

But . . . . had it all been a bit TOO easy? The idea had perhaps been too good. Suddenly Letterland was having problems. With so many Magic Endings showering sparks on to **a**pples and **o**ranges and **i**nk bottles and **u**mbrellas, they were all disappearing from words! Even worse, whenever one of them disappeared, a Vowel Man HAD to appear and say his name. Suddenly the Vowel Men were having to play the Naming Game all the time – even when they didn't WANT to!

"Help!" cried Mr E. "My lovely Naming Game is working TOO well! What shall I do? I can't undo Magic. Once I make an ending Magic, it *stays* Magic!" For once he could see no **eee**asy way out.

"Help! Help! Help! Help!" cried the **a**pples and **o**ranges and **i**nk bottles and **u**mbrellas. "We don't WANT to disappear in all these showers of sparks. We don't WANT the Vowel Men taking our places all the time. Lots of words NEED us for our SOUNDS. They don't need the Vowel Men saying their NAMES!"

tap

tapped

tapping

In the end it was Mr O (who is very old and wise) who solved the problem, simply by asking Mr E one question. "Can Magic Sparks ever jump back over more than one letter?"
"No!" cried Mr E.

"Then all we need," said Mr O slowly, "is to bring in a Best Friend to the rescue!"

Discuss what Mr O might mean. Lead the children to discover that the doubled letter puts the short vowel out of reach. The Magic Sparks are not strong enough to reach over *two* letters — only over *one*. So this is how to STOP the Magic! Put another letter in between: not just any letter, because the word does not need a new sound. Another letter of the same kind is the perfect answer, sharing the sound and warding off the sparks.
See Chart displays, page 22.

Short Vowel Symbol   At this point the short vowel drawing which the children made earlier (see p 45) will be useful. Bring out, through play-acting, the special responsibility of any final consonant to protect any short vowel by watching out for Magic Endings (just as the alert speller must do).

The moment a Magic Ending comes in sight the final letter calls, "Friend to the Rescue!" The Best Friend should arrive immediately to block the sparks, using a halting gesture. Support your play-acting with the Rescue song (Letterland Songbook and Audio Tape 2B).

In hundreds of words the vowel needs protection before a Magic Ending. Advise the children to 'put on their brakes' before they add **ed**, **ing** or any other Magic Ending to a word. Listen first to their vowel: sound or name? If they hear a vowel sound, quick, protect it!

tan	wed	chip	nod	drum
tanned	wedded	chipped	nodded	drummed
tanning	wedding	chipping	nodding	drumming
pad	net	pin	top	rub
padded	netted	pinned	topped	rubbed
padding	netting	pinning	topping	rubbing
clap	beg	trim	trot	stun
clapped	begged	trimmed	trotted	stunned
clapping	begging	trimming	trotting	stunning
wag	fret	fib	rob	strut
wagged	fretted	fibbed	robbed	strutted
wagging	fretting	fibbing	robbing	strutting

Other useful words for practising blocking the Magic Sparks from **ed** and **ing**:

bragged

brag	drip	fit	prod	sag	slip	tag
clip	drop	nag	ram	scan	stop	tap
clot	flag	peg	rib	skip	strap	trim
dip	flop	pet	rig	slap	strip	wrap

Magic en Makes Vowel Men Appear

awaken	even	liken	outspoken	siren	token
broken	forsaken	mistaken	raven	spoken	widen
Eden	frozen	omen	ripen	stolen	whiten
enliven	laden	open	shaken	taken	woven

Magic en's Sparks are Blocked

bedridden	forgotten	kitten	mitten	sadden	sudden
bitten	gladden	lessen	pollen	sodden	sullen
fatten	happen	happen	redden	smitten	trodden
forbidden	hidden	madden	rotten	stiffen	written

> **Picture code each en and Vowel Man**

1. The raven had even stolen the mitten.
2. They will widen that hidden road.
3. That gate is rotten and broken.

Not cc but ck The hard **c** is seldom doubled. Instead of calling in Clever Cat's country cousin, **cc**, the King himself comes to the vowel's rescue: **ck** e.g. bla**ck**en, bra**ck**en, chi**ck**en, qui**ck**en, sla**ck**en, si**ck**en. Exception: so**cc**er.

Sometimes not **ss** but **st** takes up the protecting role. In these words Ticking Tess has come very quickly and quietly to the rescue: chri**st**en, fa**st**en, gli**st**en, ha**st**en and li**st**en.

Magic est Makes Vowel Men Appear

bravest	finest	nicest	ripest	stalest
closest	lamest	palest	tamest	widest
cutest	latest		safest	wisest

Magic est's Sparks are Blocked

biggest	fattest	flattest	reddest	thinnest
dimmest	fittest	maddest	slimmest	wettest

> **Picture code each est and Vowel Man**

1. He was the biggest as well as the tamest of tigers.
2. The wisest man is also the fittest one.
3. The latest fad is the maddest of all.

The nicest man is the fattest one.

Magic Sparks Already Out of Reach

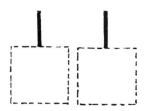

As soon as we ask children to focus on double consonants there is a risk that they will start doubling consonants everywhere. Point out that there is no need to double up when two consonants are already in the way.

act	ended	soften	eldest
acted	resting	freshen	fondest
acting	thinking	silken	bluntest

Do Not Protect Vowel Men

There is also a risk that the Magic Sparks will be blocked by mistake. Play-act some long vowel words to make it clear that hearing a Vowel *Name* in a word is a clear indication *not* to double the consonant. Otherwise the Vowel Man will disappear, whether we like it or not. Act out the result: **hāted** would become **hătted**, **cōned/cŏnned**, **elōped/elŏpped**, etc.

hated	debated	coned	fading	sliding	eloping
skated	filed	cubed	rating	pining	tubing

Right or Wrong?   Use the examples below to show how the children can check their own spelling before a Magic Ending. Is a second consonant right or wrong? With older children you may wish to skip or adapt the 'Best Friend to the Rescue' story to their interest level. With or without it, they can still benefit from this picture coding exercise. Box the ending, shoot the sparks over and add the stick man, or show the blocked sparks and code the protected vowel sound.

strapped	piped	joged
knoted	kidnaped	flogged
strutted	grabbed	flaped
slaming	combinning	yaping
strutting	glidding	begining
skiping	exploding	blaming

Exceptions   Delay this information, as relatively few words that could cause spelling difficulties fall into this group. Short vowels only need protection when the accent is on the final syllable. So *if*, in longer words, the accent is on an earlier syllable no double consonant is need. e.g. fi**tt**ed but prófited, fi**tt**ing but prófiting, lo**pp**ed but devéloped.

Note.   Magic Endings never fire back on each other. Therefore in rip en ing or, for example, happen, happen ed no second **n** is needed to protect **en** from a further Magic Ending.

Clever Cat and Kicking King

How to spell the initial "k.." sound: **c**? or **k**? Fortunately **c** and **k** are very different shapes, although alike in sound. As children learn the general look of words it usually becomes

apparent whether **c** or **k** looks right at the start of a word. If in doubt the uncertain speller should know that the odds are heavily in favour of **c**, unless the next letter is an **e** or **i**. To spell a final " . . .k"sound is

more difficult. When should it be -**c**? When -**k**, when -**ck** or -**ke**? Generally speaking four guidelines cover the use of **c**, **k**, -**ck** and -**ke**.

The Cat and the King Finish Short, Quick Words Together

The cat loves watching the Kicking King practise his kicks at the end of short, qui**ck** words, where he does most of his really big ki**ck**s. Over 85 useful 'short, qui**ck**' (short vowel one-syllable) words end in **ck**.

sack peck kick clock stuck

back	check	brick	block	buck
black	deck	chick	dock	duck
crack	fleck	flick	flock	luck
pack	peck	thick	lock	suck
track	speck	trick	smock	truck

The King Alone Says "K . . ." in Magic e Words

When you hear a Vowel Man saying his name just before a **k** . . . sound, the chances are that Magic Sparks are landing on him from a Magic **e**. These sparks jump back over only one letter, the Kicking King alone.

Why do no words end in **-cke**? Because the Cat is afraid the Magic Sparks might land on her, so she hides whenever a Magic **e** is placed beside the Kicking King, e.g. ba**ck** but ba**ke**, li**ck** but li**ke**, smo**ck** but smo**ke**, du**ck** but du**ke**.

take like joke duke

awake	mistake	alike	pike	broke	smoke
bake	shake	bike	spike	choke	stroke
lake	take	dislike	strike	joke	duke
make	quake	like	awoke	poke	fluke

Picture code each ck and ke

1. Thick smoke can make you cry
2. It is luck to strike good fortune twice.

The King Alone Says "K . . ." After Two Vowels

Clever Cat stays away from the Boot and Foot twins and Vowel Men Out Walking because she is frightened of being stepped on. So do not expect to see her in her usual place beside the King.

Did he speak to the spook?

book	look	took	weak	peek	oak	break
cook	shook	leak	cheek	seek	croak	steak
hook	spook	speak	Greek	week	soak	streak

(There are very few others.)

In All Other Words, If in Doubt Choose Clever Cat

Clever Cat is proud to *begin* far more words than the Kicking King because the King finds kicking too cramped at the start of words. (For proof compare the size of the **c** and **k** sections of any dictionary.)

Clever Cat also turns up far more often than the King *inside* words.

Clever Cat proudly *finishes* longer words all by herself (virtually all two or more syllable words).

Exploding Letters

The various functions of the apostrophe are not easy to teach – witness the large number of literate adults who get it wrong. Possibly **do'nt** for **don't** is the most frequent error, where the writer is not aware that the apostrophe should mark the place of a missing letter and its missing sound, not the space between two words compounded into one.

Hopefully, the concept of Exploding Letters will help prevent these errors. Plan a time gap between teaching 'Exploding Letters' and the 'Belonging Peg Comma' section (page 67). Let necessity determine which section to teach first. Higher usage suggests that 'Exploding Letters' will come first. (No Picture Code Card provided.)

A Broken Bit Marks the Spot Where the Explosion Took Place.

Sometimes, when we speak quickly, the words tumble out of our mouths so fast that they bump into each other. When you see these words written down, the parts *you can no longer hear* will have disappeared. What has happened to them? They have exploded! For example, if you want to say "I do not!" quickly, you say "I **don't**". The words **do** and **not** bump together so hard that the **o** in **not** explodes, turning **do not** into **don't**. Although the explosion is very quiet it is so great that most of the broken bits are never seen again.

Strangely enough, one of the exploded pieces (but only one) always comes floating down to hover over the spot where the explosion took place. This broken bit marking the spot looks like a piece of an **o**, but you never know. It might be a bit of some other letter, because **o** is not the only letter which explodes when **it's** bumped.

If you want to say "**I am** . . ." quickly, you say "**I'm** . . .". Listen: **I'm**. Which letter explodes? The **a** explodes!

I am ⟶ I'm

If you want to say "**that is** . . ." quickly, you will say "**that's** . . .". Which letter explodes this time? The **i** explodes!

that is ⟶ that's

If you want to say "**Let us** . . ." quickly, you will say "**Let's** . . .". Which letter explodes? The **u** explodes!

Let us ⟶ Let's

Sometimes more than one sound disappears, so more than one letter explodes. Even then, only one broken bit is ever seen again. Its job, it seems, is to mark the place where several explosions took place. Sometimes the first half of the word **have** explodes: **I've**.

$$I \text{ have} \longrightarrow I\text{'ve}$$

Sometimes the first half of the word **will** explodes: **I'll**.

$$I \text{ will} \longrightarrow I\text{'ll}$$

The biggest explosions may include three or four letters or even a whole word. If you want to say "**I would like it**" quickly, you will say "**I'd like it**." There is not much left of **would** after that explosion!

$$I \text{ would} \longrightarrow I\text{'d}$$

When we say "**o'clock**" we really mean "**of the clock**". So not only **f** but all letters in the word **the** explode too!

$$of \text{ the clock} \longrightarrow o\text{'clock}$$

don't	hasn't	isn't	won't	can't	it's	he'd	she'll
doesn't	haven't	wasn't	wouldn't	couldn't	that's	you'd	we'll
didn't	hadn't	weren't	shouldn't	mustn't	what's	you've	they'll

it is → it's
(as expected)

its = belonging to it
(exception)

Take Care: **it is** becomes **it's**, but **its** means 'belonging to'. The only reason **its** has no 'Belonging Peg Comma' is because it would then look exactly like **it is** after the **i** has exploded.

It's a pity the dog cut (its) paw.

you are → you're

your = belonging to you

Again Take Care The words **you're** and **your** sound alike. The broken bit shows which one is really two words bumped together.

You're (your) own worst enemy.

The Boot And Foot Twins

Mr O, the Old Man from over the ocean (long **o**), Oscar Orange (short **o**) and Oscar's Bothersome Little Brother (**o** as in br**o**ther) were all introduced in 'First Steps'. Now it is time to look at what happens when two **o**'s appear together in a word. Meet the B**oo**t and F**oo**t Twins! The fun and mischief in these twins comes out best in the Boot and Foot Twin song (Letterland Songbook 2B). The refrain reinforces the two sounds of **oo**. Even if you prefer to focus on one Twin's sound at first, it will not hurt to teach the song early on. The second sound can 'lie fallow' in the children's auditory memory until you are ready to give it fuller attention.

The Boot and Foot Twins Always Fight Over Their Boots

These twins are the two grandsons of Mr O, the Old Man. They spend so much time fighting over their b**oo**ts that everybody calls them the "B**oo**t and F**oo**t Twins". In most words you will hear the first twin, the B**oo**t Twin, teasing his brother by saying "OO, I have your b**oo**ts!"

Sometimes instead you will hear the second twin, the F**oo**t Twin, complaining, "O̬O̬, just l**oo̬**k at my f**oo̬**t!"

(The second sound is on the reverse side of the Picture Code Card, as shown by the small number two in the top right corner.)

afternoon	choose	igloo	moose	root	stool
baboon	cocoon	kangaroo	noodles	school	swoop
balloon	cool	loot	proof	shampoo	too
bamboo	droop	maroon	racoon	shoot	tool
bloom	fool	macaroon	roost	soon	tooth
boot	goose	moon	room	stool	spoons
booth	hoop	moo	rooster	spook	zoo

bedroom	cook	good	likelihood	overtook	withstood
book	childhood	goodness	look	rook	wood
brook	crook	hood	mushroom	soot	wool
broom	crooked	hook	nook	stood	woollen

Picture code each oo

1. He is in too bad a mood to eat good food.
2. I feel like a fool in this wool hat.

Six alternative spellings for the **oo** sound: 'D**o** y**ou** want t**o** u**se** that n**ew** bl**ue** br**ew** of fr**ui**t j**ui**ces?'

Luckily most words *are* spelt with **oo**. Those which are not can be learnt in small groups (see Link Words, page 32). For children who notice the **oo** sound in a word like **do** and ask "What has happened to the second twin?", the next story explains.

Sometimes the Foot Twin Hides Behind the Boot Twin

In a few words you will have both Twins but see only one. There are two reasons. Sometimes the Foot Twin likes to play peek-a-b**oo**. Then he hides behind his brother while the Boot Twin says "**oo**", as usual.

To and fro. What a to-do !

At other times the Foot Twin hides behind his brother because he is afraid of the Wicked Water Witch. Again the Boot Twin says "**oo**", as usual.

Who will be first to lose a loose tooth?

	do	disapprove	lose	prove	two	who
	doer	into	move	remove	undo	whose
	doing	lasso	overdo	to	unto	whom

(There are not many others.)

Exceptions: y**ou**, s**ou**p, gr**ou**p, tr**ou**pe, r**ou**te.

For help in spelling **you** see Starter Pack Code Sheet 31.

Vowel Men Out Walking

This rule makes a vast number of new words decodable by the still inexperienced reader. The child who has learned to read **rain** is usually unable to read **aim**, **raid**, **faint** or any other less familiar words containing **ai**. Suddenly all these new words can be made accessible. The same will apply to the four other vowel pairs, **ay**, **oa**, **ee**, and **ea**. Your children's reading vocabulary will expand dramatically once they know the 'Vowels out Walking' principle. They illustrate it by adding their own stick men right through each vowel pair. They draw the outside hand of the first stick man raised in greeting to show that *this* vowel man is talking. They draw the other stick man shielding his forehead to show that *he* is the silent look-out man. Study one pair at a time or **ai**, **oa**, **ee** and **ea** together, depending on the age and ability of your pupils. Leave **ay** and the second sound of **ea** until later (see below). The conventional version of the Vowel-Men-Out-Walking principle tends to be worded roughly as follows. 'When two vowels are together in a word, the sound of the first is long and the second is silent.' To make use of this rule a child must have a very adult grasp of its meaning.

By contrast, if children work from the little rhyme given below, the **ai**, **ay**, **ee**, **ea** and **oa** cards and the 'Vowel Men Out Walking' Scene, they can start to handle this major decoding strategy correctly straight away, even if they are still uncertain as to which letters are vowels, which vowels follow the rule (several vowel pairs do not), what sounds are long or short, or what the difference is between sounds and names.

When Two Vowel Men Go Out Walking the First One Does the Talking

1. When two vowels go out walking
   the FIRST man does the talking.
   He just says his name,
   But his friend won't do the same.

2. For his friend is the look-out man
   Watching out for the Robber band,
   Who catch vowels when they can
   As they walk through Letterland.

| When Mr A and I go out walking, Mr A does the talking. | When Mr E and A go out walking, Mr E does the talking. | When two E's go out walking, the first Mr E does the talking. | When Mr O and A go out walking, Mr O does the talking. |

The following list is divided into priority groups, high usage words first. Follow up by singing and miming the 'Vowels Out Walking' song, Letterland Songbook and Audio Tape 2B.

again [1]	entertain	each [1]	neat	been [1]	steel	boat [1]	coax [8]
rain	gain	eat	steam	see	referee [5]	coal [2]	cockroach
afraid [2]	rail	clean [2]	peach [6]	three	sheet	coat	encroach
train	remain	leaf	peak	trees	speech	road	foal
wait	waist	leaves	steal	between[2]	agree [6]	goal [3]	foam
mail [3]	claim [8]	meat	bean [7]	feed	coffee	soap	gloat
paid	complaint	beach [3]	cheap	green	committee	coast [4]	groan
paint	drain	beat	grease	keep	geese	load [5]	hoax
raise	faint	east	scream	seen	keen	roam	Joan
straight	frail	Easter	appeal [8]	sleep	knee	float [6]	loan
tail	maintain	mean	cheat	street	degree [7]	loaf	loathe
grain [4]	pail	teach	eager	deep [3]	heel	oatmeal	loathsome
nails	praise	bead [4]	eaten	feel	indeed	roast	moan
aim [5]	raid	cream	flea	feelings	screen	throat	moat
plain	raisin	dream	heap	feet	cheek [8]	toast	oaf
trail	refrain	heat	leak	free	deed	cloak [7]	oath
aid [6]	retain	least	lean	meet	eel	coach	poach
bait	sailing	meal	leap	need	flee	loaf	poached
daily	saint	reach	plea	queen	Greek	loaves	reproach
explain	snail	reason	repeat	seem	peel	approach	soak
fail	Spain	season	reveal	sweet	peep	boast [8]	soaking
pain	stain	speak	squeak	teeth	spree	bloated	stoat
brain [7]	vain	stream	treason	bee [4]	toffee	broach	toad
contain	wail	deal [5]	weak	seed	weed	coated	

Exception: broad. Most other exceptions are followed by **r**, see page 143.

**Observation of Detail in 'Vowel Men Out Walking'
Pictures**.   Point out on the Vowel Men Out Walking Scene that both letters of each vowel pair are in one colour to emphasize that the two letters are now making only one sound. Have everyone look carefully at both of the vowel men in a pair, to discover for themselves that the first one always has his mouth open to show that he is saying his name, and the second one, the look-out man, has his mouth shut showing that he always remains silent.

Why Is the Second Vowel Man Silent?   The answer to this question is a means of explaining the one important exception to the rule; that is, when two vowels are followed by an **r** in -**air, -ear, -eer** and -**oar**. The second Vowel Man is silent because he is too busy looking out for **r**obbers to do any talking. Robbers are dangerous, and not least because they steal the Vowel Men's belongings (see **ar, or, er, ur, ir**). They also like to capture the Vowel Men themselves, and their sounds!

It is a good idea briefly to show the exceptions in the yellow panel, but then to cover them up until the children have become skilled at handling 'the First Man Does the Talking' principle. In the meantime if an exception comes up as you hear a child read you might like to mutter, "See that **r**obber next to the Vowels Out Walking? He's trying to make this word difficult for you. We'll deal with him later." Then give the difficult word. It is enough at this point if the child knows that any **r** after a vowel pair will invalidate the usual 'Vowels Out Walking' principle.

The exceptions, see page 143.
Also page 112.

Apply the Picture Code.   In the following sentences there are only regular short vowels and 'Vowels Out Walking' so that there are no distractions from learning to spot the walking pairs.

| Picture code each a, i and ai | 1. He cannot aim his gun well in the rain. |
| | 2. I am afraid the paint has left a big stain. |

| Picture code each e, a and ea | 1. The beastly flea had eaten Ted's meat. |
| | 2. He felt eager to reach the top of the second peak. |

| Picture code each e and ee | 1. I need to see the queen next week. |
| | 2. In Greenland it seems to get very cold indeed. |

| Picture code each o, a and oa | 1. The coach approached the old moat. |
| | 2. The cockroach sat on the loaf of toasted oats. |

When Mr A and the Yo-yo Man Go Out Walking Mr A Does the Talking

When Mr A goes out walking, his favourite walking partner is Mr I who acts as a silent look-out man for them both. But when Mr A goes out walking at the *end* of a word it is no use taking Mr I with him because Mr I always feels dizzy at the end of words (see page 60). So Mr I and the Yo-yo Man have agreed that the Yo-yo Man should always take over as Mr A's look-out man at the *ends* of words.

Mr I did say that he must stay away.

archway	delay	gateway	May	ray	subway
astray	dismay	gay	midway	relay	sway
away	display	hay	mislay	repay	today
betray	doorway	hearsay	pathway	runway	tray
byway	essay	highway	play	say	way
clay	fray	jay	pray	spray	waylay
day	gangway	lay	railway	stray	yesterday

Exceptions: they, grey, obey, prey, osprey. See page 104.

| Picture code each a, ai and ay | 1. Did she say we can play with clay if it rains today? |
| | 2. The haystack is a long way from the railway tracks. |

When Mr E and Mr A Go Out Walking the Elephant May Do the Talking

When Mr E goes out walking with Mr A he sometimes gives his pet Elephant a turn with the talking. Then, instead of hearing Mr E say his name **e**xpect Eddy Elephant to say 'ĕ' for ĕlephant inst**ea**d.

Ed is ready to say "ĕa".

ahead	dead	dread	heather	jealous	meant	ready	thread
bread	deaf	feather	heaven	lead	peasant	spread	threat
breakfast	dealt	head	heavy	leather	pheasant	steady	wealth
breath	death	health	instead	meadow	pleasant	tread	weather

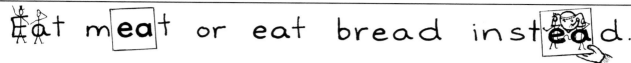

Eat m**ea**t or eat bread inst**ea**d.

r**ea**d

r**ea**d

Which Sound; ea or ea? Look for context clues first. If there are none try Mr E's name, since far more words containing **ea** saying ē than ĕ. Still no luck? Then try ĕ in case Eddy Elephant is having a turn talking. Hold up both Picture Code Cards for **ea** so that the children can decide which sound (therefore which pictogram) fits. Also set out examples with the **ea** cards plain side up. Play 'Guess the picture on the other side' by analysing the sound. Then turn the cards over to see if the picture is 'right' or 'wrong'.

Collect common words containing **ea** saying ĕ into sentences. Samples: He r**ea**d and r**ea**d until his h**ea**d was h**ea**vy as l**ea**d.

He faced d**ea**th with his w**ea**pon r**ea**dy.

> **Picture code each ea and ea**

1. Please leave things ready for breakfast.
2. Treat his threat as a mean joke.

gr**ea**t

h**ay**stack

s**ea**g**u**ll

unl**oa**d

ox**tai**l

w**ee**k**e**nd

Exceptions: br**ea**k, gr**ea**t and st**ea**k. These are the only common words in which Mr A actually has a turn at doing the talking, instead of Mr E or his Elephant.

'Vowels Out Walking' and Short Vowels The phrases give reading and spelling practice in Vowels Out Walking plus regular short vowel sounds, so that the children learn to switch from the short to the long vowel sounds with ease.

At a later date you may wish to use some of these same examples again mixed with Magic E words, or with any other sound you are currently teaching or revising.

> **Picture code single vowels and Vowels Out Walking**

subway	cheap trip	payment	loaded
increase	seventeen	peaches	cleanest
freedom	explaining	essay	approach
containing	at least	sweeten	fleeting

AI, OA, EE and EA Out Walking

At l**ea**st w**ai**t for the fl**ee**t to s**ai**l by the c**oa**st.

oak tree	cheap roast	neat and clean	three train loads
green pea	soapy foam	need to explain	reach for a peach
main road	rainy season	eaten a meal	boasting claim
queen bees	sixteen loaves	straight street	afraid of toads
brain drain	peach peel	cheat and steal	seems to feel
deep seas	painted leaves	plain speaking	weak at the knees

failing to pay	for reasons of health	at least as steady
no complaints today	meat and bread	speak with ease
explain it again	peasant's meal	meant to please
stay waiting	leapt from his seat	the threat of death

Vowels Out Walking Plus a Magic e or Magic Ending   Many words contain both Vowels Out Walking and a Magic **e** or Magic Ending. Such words will seem much too long and difficult to inexperienced readers until they have learned to decode them. Once they can, again the number of words which they can work out for themselves is increased many fold. The first examples above and below combine short vowel syllables with Vowels Out Walking. Subsequent examples point up the frequency of both Vowels Out Walking words and Magic **e** words in our language. Often both structures occur within one word.

fine gateway	nice meal	heavy fine	painted snake
meanwhile we hope	free display	peaches in wine	three white geese
keep eels on ice	quite painless	bite his coat	on the roadside
teenage fun	combine the teams	choking on peas	a decade away

mealtime   cheesecake   railway

railroad   deadline   headway

teenage   meanwhile   trainload

Make up menus with Magic **e** and Vowels out Walking words:

Poached Egg on Toast	Roast Beef with Peas	Tea and Cake
Bread with Marmalade	Rice or Baked Beans	Ice Cream
Tea or Coffee	Peaches and Cream	Sweets

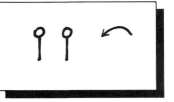

Abbreviate the Picture Code   Once the principles are well understood abbreviate the picture code for the sake of speed, as per examples below. As soon as the words become easy to analyse without superimposing any drawings drop the picture coding altogether. It will have served its purpose.

speedboat   seaweed   brainwave

limestone   gateway   raincoat   daydream

drainpipe   teenage   seaside   meantime

beehive   milestone   waistcoat

PLEASE KEEP FEET OFF THESE SEATS

breathless   deadlock   dreadful

96

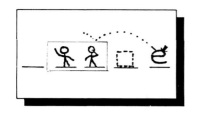

Magic e Never Lands on Vowel Men Out Walking   Some children become so adept at spotting Magic **e**'s, and other Magic Endings, that they try to apply the 'Magic' principle to *two* vowels as well as to any preceding *single* vowel. At this point it is important that they learn that 'even Magic Sparks can't make the look-out man his silence break.' The same fact applies not only to Vowel Men Out Walking, but to any other two vowels making one sound, e.g. **oo, ou, oi** and **au**. To emphasize the point the children can put the two vowels into a protective box and show how the Magic Sparks just bounce off it instead of making the nearest vowel say its name.

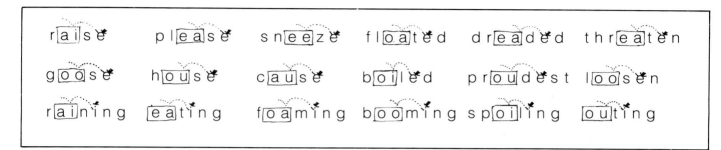

When Other Vowel Men Walk the First One May Talk

doe, hoe toe potatoes tomatoes	nuisance pursuit suit	argue rescue avenue tissue	people

Sometimes the Second Vowel Man Talks Too

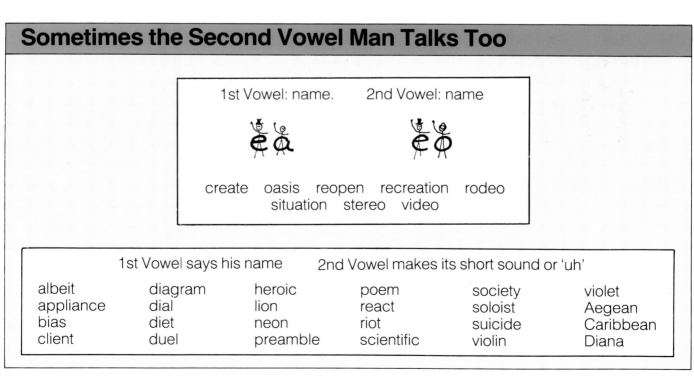

1st Vowel: name.   2nd Vowel: name

create   oasis   reopen   recreation   rodeo
situation   stereo   video

1st Vowel says his name			2nd Vowel makes its short sound or 'uh'		
albeit	diagram	heroic	poem	society	violet
appliance	dial	lion	react	soloist	Aegean
bias	diet	neon	riot	suicide	Caribbean
client	duel	preamble	scientific	violin	Diana

IE and EI Out Walking See Page 141.

Spelling Hints for 'Vowels out Walking' Words   Who usually walks with whom? Mr A nearly always prefers Mr I to act as his look-out man *inside* words. Mr I rarely goes out walking with anyone except Mr E as his look-out man.

Mr O usually goes out walking with Mr A because they are both fruit growers! In a few words Mr O goes out walking with Mr E instead (e.g. goes, hoe, toe, etc.) but then what is happening in words like *does* or *shoe* and *canoe*?

Breaking the rule (children love breaking rules) is another good way to remember a few silent look-out men. Make the silent look-out men talk by pronouncing the word **Tuesday** as "Tu-ē-sday" and **people** as "pe-ō-ple".

Pain or Pane?   When asking children to spell a word like **pain** by ear you should hint, "This is not going to be a Magic **e** word, so who is Mr A most likely to choose as his silent look-out man?" If the children cannot remember the usual partner, let them check for themselves on the Vowel Men Out Walking Scene or mime them. Gradually they will remember the most used pairs, reducing the amount of rote memory work otherwise needed to master the spelling of a large number of Vowels Out Walking words.

Which Spelling: EE? or EA?   Whether Mr E is out walking with Mr A (**ēa**) or his brother (**ēe**) is more difficult, but once the words **see**, **seem**, **been**, **meet**, **green**, **queen** and the **'teens** are familiar, the odds are heavily in favour of **ea**.

Most Used EE Words   Each concrete word in this group could be coloured green in paintings, as an added reminder that, like the word **green**, they are all spelt with **ee**.

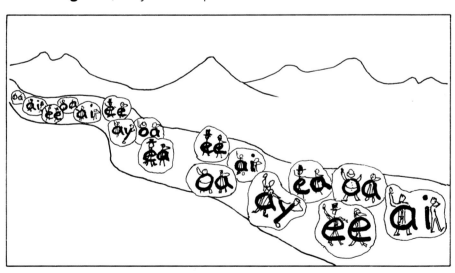

Follow Up   Make a mural with a long road full of Vowel Men Out Walking. Smaller pictures at the left, getting bigger towards the right, will create a real sense of perspective. You can also add speech bubbles with one Vowel-out-Walking word in each bubble.

Giant All & Giant Full

Both single **l** and double **ll** can signal a change in the sound of either an **a** or **u** before it. What happens to the **a**pple? What happens to the **u**mbrella? And why sometimes one **l**, sometimes two?

The Letterland explanations introduce two towering giants, Giant **All** and Giant **Full**, one greedy and one good. Use them to heighten attention to the **all**, **al** and **full**, **ful** spelling patterns and to create a logic for the otherwise uninteresting

'drop one **l** before/after a root word' rules which govern **al-** and **-ful**. The challenge is to watch out for these big giants and learn what they are up to in words!

Giant All Eats Almost All the Apples He Can Find

Giant **All** is so **tall** that **all** you can see of him in words is his two **l**ong **l**egs. In fact his legs alone are as long as the Lamp Lady is **tall**! How can you tell when he appears in a word?

The secret lies in knowing Giant **All**'s one great weakness. He has a passion for **a**pples! He is so fond of Letterland **a**pples that he just strides into words and grabs them - without asking. This makes the people of Letterland very angry.

They call him 'Giant **Al**most **All**', because he grabs **al**most **all** the **a**pples he can find. So if you see a word with an **a**pple in it and then two straight lines right beside it, the chances are that you have spotted the two **l**ong **l**egs of Giant **All**.

When you do, don't expect the **a**pple to be saying **ă**, because Giant **All** will be eating that **a**pple! Can you hear him saying "**all**" in these words?

The tallest man of all is Giant All.

	Giant **All** eating all the **a**pples he can find.			
	all	fall	recall	downfall
	ball	fallen	smallest	eyeball
	befall	hall	stall	forestall
	call	hallmark	tall	holdall
	called	install	taller	rainfall
	calling	pitfall	wall	snowball
	enthrall	small	walls	waterfall

	A few **a**pples he has missed.	
	Allan	challenge
	alley	Hallowe'en
	alligator	Sally
	ballad	valley

Picture code ă, l, ll and all

1. Sally thinks that Giant All is appallingly tall.
2. Twelve men walled in the small plot of land very well.

Giant All Leans on Other Words Because He is Lazy

Giant **All** really is a lazy old giant. If he can find another word to lean on while he eats, he will. Being so **tall** he just reaches over, pulls up a word, and leans right back on it. The lazy old giant likes leaning far better than standing on his own two feet.

When Giant **All** is leaning on a word you won't see both of his legs because one is just behind the other. But don't let that fool you. It is still Giant **All**. Most of **all** Giant **All** likes to lean on the words **most**, **so**, and **ways**. His next most favourite words are **ready** and **though**.

 all but  almost

also always already although

altogether almighty albeit

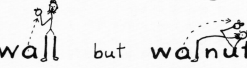 wall but walnut

In a few words he even manages to make do by leaning on just a piece of a word, instead of a whole one.

 bald

| altar | bald | halt | malt | asphalt |
| alter | scald | halter | malted | Walter |

Apple and Lamp Lady As Usual   Luckily Giant **All** does not get **all** of the **a**pples. Quite a few words still have an **a**pple and the Lamp Lady in them as usual.

 album

| album | algebra | altitude | calender | salad |
| alcohol | alphabet | balance | palace | value |

Giant All Mural   A school staircase is a good place for a Giant All display with Giant All towering up from the bottom step reaching for apples in the top of a tree half way up. Younger children might provide 'Apple Words' (with regular **a**) while your class adds words coded with Giant All.

Words Ending in - al   When **al** becomes a suffix it sounds different, see page 133.

Parachuted Apples   What has happened to the **a**pples in a few words like **a**like, **a**live, **a**long, **a**loud? See page 145.

100

Giant Full Says "Full" As He Fills U Full of Umbrellas

The other giant who lives in Letterland is Giant **Full**. Unlike Giant All who does not help matters at **all**, Giant **Full** is a very help**ful** fellow. He loves helping Mr U by filling his **u**'s **full** of **u**mbrellas for him. In fact Mr U calls him "Giant Fill-**U-Full**" because he fills so many **u**'s **full** of **u**mbrellas! The only trouble is that, as he fills the **u**'s **full** he shouts out '**full**' so loudly in his deep giant's voice, you cannot hear the **u**mbrella's sound anymore! This can make **full** sound like a difficult word to spell; but not if you think to yourself, 'What letter would Giant Full fill so **full** of **u**mbrellas. It must be **u**!'

That *ů* is almost f*ů*ll !

Giant Full Leans On Other Words Whenever He Can

It seems that apart from helping Mr U Giant **Full** is even lazier than Giant **All**. To prove the point just look at the number of words he leans on. He leans on so many that he hardly ever stands on his own two feet, except in the one word **full**. When he leans on another word you won't see his second leg because one leg is behind the other.

cupful	neglectful	skilful	grateful	boastful
eventful	plentiful	tactful	hateful	disdainful
forgetful	pitiful	thankful	hopeful	faithful
handful	restful	wishful	shameful	painful
hatful	respectful	wistful	spiteful	peaceful
helpful	sinful	wonderful	useful	playful
fanciful	armful	awful	beautiful	Also: fulfil
forceful	artful	lawful	cheerful	fulsome
merciful	harmful	doubtful	glassful	fulness
successful	purposeful	mouthful	spoonful	
fearful	careful	delightful	truthful	
tearful	thoughtful	frightful	youthful	

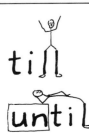

Picture code each full and ful

1. Be careful of those full baskets.
2. He was grateful for a handful of pennies.

In -**ful** words plus -**ly**, the second **l** is the Lamp Lady.

One More Giant   There is a *third* giant in Letterland called Giant **Till** but people rarely see him because he only appears in two words. They are **till** and (when he turns sideways) **until**. Can you imagine what he looks like and draw him in those two words?

The Yo-yo Man's Business Deals with Mr E

Since pronunciation varies in different regions, some teachers will prefer to present the unaccented **y** at the end of words as a short **i** sound, not a long **e** sound. If so, use only the page 62 picture coding and story. Before making this decision, however, observe your children's spelling mistakes, e.g. **baby** spelt **babi** or **babe**, **softly** spelt **sofli** or **softle**. Most teachers find that **e** is chosen because the child says "babee, softlee", etc. in an effort to hear and identify the final sound. The other common mis-spelling is **-ey**, e.g. **softley**. Show any child who has an **-ey** habit the list on page 104 giving the very few words that really *do* end in **-ey**. By contrast there are several *thousand* words which end in **y** sounding like **e**. Picture coding will help. The child simply draws a tiny **e** in the Yo-yo Man's sack instead. of mis-spelling the word.

The Yo-yo Man's Biggest and Best Business Deal

Much as the Yo-yo Man enjoys working for Mr I he needs more work than Mr I can give him. Luckily the Yo-yo Man has another friend who needs help. It is Mr E.

Do you remember Mr E's special invention for the end of words, his silent Magic **e**, which works so well for playing the Naming Game? (See page 68). Well, he quite forgot that in many, many words people just do not want an **e** to become silent at the end.

There was nothing Mr E could do to change his Silent **e**'s back into **e**'s which could still say **ē**. In fact his magic had worked so well that now nearly any **e** that *anyone* puts at the end of a word *automatically* turns into a Silent **e**! What could Mr E do? He was rushing about in a terrible state until he saw the Yo-yo Man.

"Can you say **ē** for me?", he cried desperately.

"I don't know," said the Yo-yo Man slowly. He put down his yo-yos and took a deep breath. Then he said "**ē**" quite easil**y**.

Mr E was ever so pleased. Immediatel**y** he gave the Yo-yo Man the job of saying **ē** for him in nearl**y** ever**y** word which *sounds* as though it ends in **ē**. So now the Yo-yo Man earns a ver**y** good living indeed, because there are not just hundreds but thousands of words where he can say **ē** for Mr E. Mr E has given him a tin**y** little **ē**, too, which he can carr**y** with him to show everybod**y** how man**y** words he finishes for Mr E.

The Yo-yo Man likes to carry the tiny e.

Mummy	clumsy	enemy	frosty	marry	pity	sorry
Daddy	colony	envy	handy	melody	plenty	sticky
balcony	company	every	hungry	merry	risky	study
berry	copy	family	hurry	milky	rocky	sulky
body	dusky	fifty	husky	misty	scratchy	tricky
brandy	dusty	filthy	inky	monopoly	seventy	ugly
carry	empty	fishy	lily	musty	sixty	windy

Anthony	Harry	Johnny	Mandy	Peggy	Sally	Germany
Bobby	Henry	Kitty	Mary	Percy	Timothy	Hungary
Emily	Ivy	Lenny	Nancy	Polly	Tony	Italy

(and many more names)

already	busy	dirty	history	only	ready
any	city	easy	juicy	party	story
anybody	country	heavy	nearly	pretty	truly

Also all adverbs ending in **-ly** (see below).

Exceptions: Words ending in **-key**, **-ley** and **-ney** (see page 104).

(see page 104).

Picture code each e and y

1. His enemy went into the empty cave.
2. His hobby is studying family history.

Lamp Lady and Yo-yo Man Together Say "lee"

Happi**ly** a great many words end in **-ly**. This makes the Lamp Lady and the Yo-yo Man very happy indeed, because she loves lighting up words and he is very pleased to work for Mr E. So they appear together most willing**ly** at the end of thousands of words.

It is lovely that they both say "-ly" so gladly.

abruptly	clearly	ghostly	kingly	rapidly	softly
badly	dimly	gladly	madly	sadly	solidly
blandly	exactly	grandly	manly	sensibly	splendidly
bluntly	flatly	hotly	oddly	shockingly	suddenly
bubbly	fondly	invisibly	promptly	sickly	willingly

and over four thousand further adverbs!

Picture code each vowel y and ly

1. That ugly frog is hopping quickly.
2. Exactly why did Tommy suddenly feel shy?

Spelling the -ly Sound Inexperienced spellers often write **le** when they should be writing **-ly**. In fact **-le** has a completely different sound ("ul") as in cand**le** (see page 131). Once you have introduced the pictogram for **-le** you can have a laugh together with any child who writes, for example, bad**le** for bad**ly** by pronouncing it "bad-ul". You can also point out that the **e** at the end must be wrong, because **e**'s automatically go silent at the end of words. Who, then, would Mr E probably ask to do the job of saying **ē** for him? The Yo-yo Man, of course! Compare **ly** and **le** on their Flap Charts.

Don't Drop Silent e Before -ly

There is no Magic in the **-ly** ending, so do not drop a Magic **e** before you add **-ly** or your Vowel Man will disappear! Instead keep **e** so that the Vowel Man can go on playing the Naming Game. The Lamp Lady and the Yo-yo Man will enjoy watching the sparks fly.

Snow has looked extremely likely lately.

Note.   Don't drop even a burnt out Magic **e** before **-ly**, e.g. not **lovly**, **surly**, **activly** but **lovely**, **surely**, **actively**.

acutely	completely	homely	likely	namely	princely	shapely	untimely
bravely	extremely	lamely	lonely	nicely	rudely	solely	widely
closely	finely	lately	mutely	politely	safely	timely	wisely

> **Picture code each each Magic e, y and ly**

1. The lonely lady shyly left to go home.
2. He spoke quietly and very politely.

Mr E and the Yo-yo Man's Journey

Mr E has given the Yo-yo Man the job of saying "**e**" at the ends of most words, more than 5,000, in fact! But in just a **few** words (about 20) instead of paying the Yo-yo Man to do work for him Mr E takes the Yo-yo Man on a journ**ey**. As they walk along Mr E does the talking and the Yo-yo Man acts as the look-out man.

They each take some **money**

and bread and **honey** on this **journey** and a pack **donkey**.

Can you bring the rest of the **-ey** words into a story about their journ**ey**? Notice that all except sto**rey** (as in a building) end in **-key**, **-ley** or **-ney**.

(Not on a Picture Code Card or Flap Chart.)

-key	-ley	-ney	-rey	Names	
donkey*, monkey*	alley, valley*	honey*, money*	storey	Geoffrey	Shirley
hockey, jockey	barley, holey	chimney*		Godfrey	Sidney
key*, turkey	parsley, trolley	journey*		Harvey	Stanley
	pulley, volley			Humphrey	Wesley

* The starred words are the most important ones to know how to spell.

 Exceptions   A few -ey words rhyme with **-ay**: th**ey**, h**ey** and gr**ey**. Also **obey**, **prey**, **survey**, **lamprey**. All are caused by Mr Mean-E who is glad so long as you spell them wrong!

Another Look at All of the Yo-yo Man's Jobs

Revision: The Yo-Yo Man's Other Jobs   To consolidate the children's understanding of the several functions of the letter **y**, write words containing **y** on the board. Provide an ice-cream cone, ink bottle and an **e** made of stiff card. The children select and place the cone, bottle or **e** in the sack of a large mural of the Yo-yo Man, depending on which **y** sound they can hear in each example.

Next, set up a list under the heading 'The Yo-yo Man's Other Jobs'. Have the children collect and categorise words containing **y**. It will soon emerge for whom **y** works most, Mr I or Mr E.

As one child summed it up, "At least the Yo yo Man won't get tummy ache from eating too many ice creams!" There are very few common words with **y** representing long **i**. By contrast **y** represents long **e** so often that the children may well speculate that the Yo-yo Man should be able to buy his dream yacht ver**y** soon!

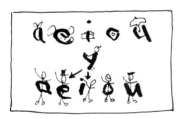

You may also like to have the children draw the vowel chart again (preferably from memory) and then add two little arrows from the Yo-yo Man's feet pointing to the Vowel Men whom he helps out in words.

Creative Writing   Suggest writing about the Yo-yo Man trying to convert an old broken down yacht in dry dock into a house boat. What problems does he find? What basic items does he need? Afterwards the children might count up the number of times they have used **y** in their stories, and which sounds those **y**'s represent.

The Wicked Witch and Robber Red

In 'First Steps' the children will have met Robber Red, symbol for the **rr**regular sound of **r** normally found at the beginning of words and in consonant blends **br**, **cr**, **dr**, etc. Although he is a **r**obber, the **Rr**ingleader in fact of a robber gang (see page 108), Robber Red himself gives little trouble to young readers in words. They can **r**ely on him to make his usual

growling sound in these consonant blend positions. In one of them, **wr**, he makes trouble for the Wicked Water Witch instead. Whenever he is next to *her* in a word he springs into action, stealing away her sound. Children have often met **wr** in words like **write**, but many do not apply the fact that **w** is silent before **r** in less familiar **wr** words. If a child starts to read

a word like **wr**eck by pronouncing the **w**, try looking startled and say, "What! How can the Witch say '**w** . . .'? Just look who is next to her! Doesn't *he* overpower *her*?" A quick look at the word and, if necessary at the **wr** Picture Code Card, confirms that Robber Red does indeed have the upper hand!

The Wicked Witch is Overpowered by Robber Red

What do you suppose might happen when the Wicked Witch and Robber Red meet each other in a word? Will the **w**itch overpower the **r**obber or will he overpower her? Try saying the word **write**. Can you hear the **w**itch? No? Can you hear Robber Red growling "**rrr . .**"? Yes? Then he must have overpowered the **w**itch! Yes, he has! Why?

Well, the Wicked Water Witch has always wanted to **wr**ite a spell against all the **r**obbers. Robber Red knows this, so every time he is within striking distance he makes sure he stops her. He rushes in, grabs her by the **wr**ist so that she can't **wr**ite, and tosses her into his sack. She is so startled that she can't speak.

Notice that Robber Red never lets any of the other **r**obbers overpower the **w**itch. He always does this most dangerous job himself. So whenever you see these two letters together who will you hear . . . ? Robber Red's triumphant growl "**rrr** . . ." as he runs along, but never a peep from the **w**itch!

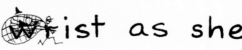 

He grabbed her **wr**ist as she **wr**ote.

(More about this story in Songbook and Audio Tape 2B)

awry	wrapping	wreckage	wretch	wrinkle	written	wry
wrap	wrath	wren	wretched	wrist	wrong	unwrap
write	wrapped	wreath	wrench	wriggle	wrote	unwrinkled
wring	wrapper	wreck	wrestle	writer	wrung	unwritten

> **Picture-code each w, wh and wr**

1. Wendy felt wretched when her dress got wrinkled.
2. Did we wrap up the wrist watch in the white box?

Eddy Elephant and the Wicked Water Witch

When Eddy Grabs Her Broomstick the Witch Cries "OO! YOU!"

When you see Eddy Elephant next to the Wicked Witch do not expect him to be saying "ĕ . . ." as usual. He will be far too busy outwitting the Witch. You see, she would love to turn him into a *wicked elephant* if she could! To make sure that she cannot, Eddy grabs away her broomstick whenever he is next to her in a word. Then she is furious because she needs her broomstick for her spells. That is why you will hear the Witch's shrill voice crying, "OO!" or "YOU!". (See **ew** Letterland Songbook and Audio Tape 2B.)

The elephant knew a few shrewd tricks.

	"OO!"			"YOU!"	
blew	flew	shrew	askew	honeydew	phew
brew	grew	shrewd	dew	interview	review
brewer	Hebrew	slew	ewe	mews	skewer
chew	Jew	strewn	few	pew	view
crew	jewel	threw	hew	pewter	yew

"OO!" or "YOU!"

new   anew   knew   news   newspaper   renewed   stew

Picture code each ew >
1. She blew the dew off the few new buds which grew.
2. We had a good view of the crew as the ship drew in.

She blew the dew off the few
new buds that grew

The Five Vowel Stealers

Whenever **r** is to the right of a vowel it changes *its* sound *and* the sound of the vowel (or any two vowels), creating the **r** controlled vowels. As a result this one letter causes endless problems for the unskilled reader. This is why all **r**'s are depicted as bad men, running robbers, out to make trouble in Letterland.

Five new pictograms symbolise the difference between the regular sound of **r** and the new sounds caused by **ar, er, ir, or** and **ur.** They are Robber Red's gang of five Vowel Stealers. Each **r**obber makes a new sound as he steals a vowel's sound. They can stop anybody from learning to read

who does not know what each **r**obber will be saying as he steals.

How can the beginner reader tell one **r** from another in a word, and remember their shifting sounds? By looking for **r**obbers with 'stolen' vowels behind their backs, and learning their surnames!

The Alphabet Name R   Children who have not begun with 'First Steps' may be calling **r** "are". Some will now need help because they confuse **r**'s alphabet name and its sound. Trying to spell words like p**ar**k and f**ar**m they omit the **a**, writing **prk, frmer,** etc. because the **ar** *sound* is identical to the **r** alphabet *name*. In fact **r** alone can *never* spell this 'ar' sound. In Letterland phrasing, never expect **R**obber **R**ed to make **Ar**thur **Ar**'s sound. Hold up the **r** and the **ar** cards showing the two quite different robber faces to emphasize the point. It is **Ar**thur **Ar**, the **a**pple stealer, who calls out his surname '**Ar**' every time he steals an **a**pple. So don't leave out the stolen **a**pple when spelling his sound!

'A' Sounding Like Alphabet Name 'R'   For help with errors such as f**ar**st, p**ar**st, **ar**fter (**f**ast, **p**ast, **a**fter) and **r**fter (**a**fter) see 'Yawning Apple Words', page 145.

Become a Detective   At this stage the children will know all the **a -z** characters. But has anyone noticed that there is not one policeman among them? The **p** is only a poor little **p**uppy with droopy ears. There are, in fact, no policemen in Letterland! So the **r**obbers can be expected to **r**un **r**iot in hundreds of words. The solution to this lawlessness, then, is for the children to become self-styled detectives. They must learn to identify every **r**obber by name, to catch each one in the act of stealing!

Add a note of drama as you introduce these wretched law breakers. The **r**obbers are even more to blame than the Wicked Witch for making reading and spelling difficult because the **r**obbers steal so often! At the same time depict them as stupid and lazy; stupid because they break the law, and lazy because they seldom bother to mend their sacks. Spot the torn netting on most **r**obber pictograms for proof that the stolen vowels always escape to turn up cheerfully in any other word that needs them!

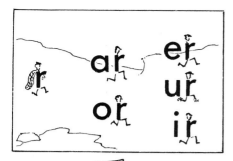

Identify the Robbers   Display the Robber Scene.

Timing   Once it is known that there is a whole band of **r**obbers, some children will want to identify 'their' **r**obbers inside their names, right away. Fine. Tell each child 'who' he or she has caught! Plan intervals between your fuller study of each Vowel Stealer to avoid confusion between their sounds. Use each Robber song on Audio Tape 2B to emphasize the differences.

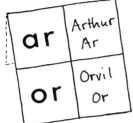

Arthur **Ar** is a convenient Vowel-Stealer to study first, especially if a few words like c**ar**, f**ar** and f**ar**m are already familiar. Have you a M**ar**k, Ch**ar**les or M**ar**garet** in your class? So much the better. The words f**or** and m**or**ning are helpful first words in which to 'discover' **Or**vil **Or**'s sound. The **Er** Broth**er**s (er/ur/ir) can be introduced later, but since **er** occurs most frequently you may wish to give **er** priority over **ur** and **ir** – perhaps over **ar** and **or** as well. Whatever your teaching order, support it with the Robber Flap Charts.

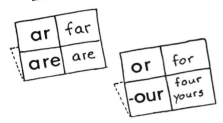

Encourage everyone playfully to over-pronounce the robbers' names and the words steal**er**, robb**er**, and broth**er**s. After all five have been 'met', follow up by letting the children make their own robber mural with each gang member behind bars, caught by your sharp-eyed readers!

Arthur AR, the Apple-Stealer

The robber who steals **a**pples (see them in his get-away c**ar**?) is **Ar**thur **Ar**. The **a**pple letter behind his back is captured. So it cannot say **ă** as usual. Instead **Ar**thur **Ar** reports back to Robber Red with a tiny walkie-talkie hidden inside his outstretched **ar**m. He calls in with just one word: his surname, "**Ar**!" Listen carefully. How many times can you hear **Ar**thur **Ar** saying "**Ar**!" in this sentence?

That robber p**ar**ks his c**ar** in the d**ar**k.

arm	bar	cart	far	jar	part	sparse	starving
armed	barred	carve	farm	lard	party	star	target
army	barb	charm	farmer	lark	pardon	start	unarmed
art	barbed	chart	garden	larch	regard	stark	upstart
artist	bark	dark	hard	mark	remark	shark	varnish
are	barn	darling	hardly	market	scar	sharp	yard

** **Ar**chibald, **Ar**chie, **Ar**nold, **Ar**thur, **Bar**bara*, **Bar**tholomew, **Ch**arles, **Ch**arlotte, M**ar**garet*, M**ar**cella, M**ar**k, M**ar**tha, M**ar**tin. (*For starred names see page 31 .)

**Picture code each
a, r and ar**

1. The army bombarded the tanks in the darkness.
2. Ann's scarf is a dark shade of scarlet.

♩ ♪ ♫
. . . Catch him, catch him
if you can, for Arthur
Ar is a very bad man!

The Apple Stealer Song   Follow up with the **Ar**thur **Ar** song (Letterland Songbook and Audio Tape 2B). If each child writes down the song in large enough handwriting to overwrite and picture code the **ar**'s in contrasting colours, as they all sing the words their attention will be repeatedly caught by the **ar** sound and spelling pattern.

The ar Sound in Dart   Play-period suggestion. Each child makes a paper d**ar**t showing **Ar**thur **Ar** d**ar**ting along in the word d**ar**t. Of course the children always want to see how f**ar** the d**ar**t will fly. A chalk line may be labelled St**ar**ting Line. Each child writes his name on a c**ar**d and: 'This c**ar**d is my m**ar**ker. My d**ar**t went this f**ar**.' Then compete to see which d**ar**t goes f**ar**thest.

Starting Line

Arthur Ar Next to Magic E

In the *one* word **are**, **Ar**thur **Ar** is reporting one more **a**pple stolen by saying '**ar**', as usual. But he is also having to grab Silent Magic **e**'s wand and break it, so that its sparks won't shoot over his head and make his stolen **a**pple disappear!

We are watching!

Are you?

In all *other* words, where you see **Ar**thur **Ar** plus a Magic **e**, the Apple Stealer c**are**fully prep**are**s to sn**are** both the **a**pple letter and the Silent Magic **e** in two sacks. He does this very r**are**ly because the letters are heavy – so heavy that as he runs off with them he puffs out hot *air*. So bew**are**! When these three letters do not sound like '**ar**' expect them to sound just like the word '**air**'.

Take care. Beware!

aware	blare	dare	glare	rare	stare
bare	care	declare	hare	scared	silverware
barefoot	careless	fare	nightmare	snare	warfare
beware	compare	flare	prepare	square	welfare

Orvil Or, the Orange-Stealer

The **r**obber who steals the **o**ranges is **Or**vil **Or**, the **o**range stealer. When an **o**range has just been stolen do not expect it to say **ŏ** for **ŏ**range any more. Once it is in **Or**vil **Or**'s sack all you will be able to hear is **Or**vil **Or** rep**or**ting back to headquarters to rec**or**d his robbery with one word, his surname, "**Or**!" **Or**vil **Or** carries an oar with him from his get-away boat by the sh**or**e. Why? So that nobody will row away with his boat while he is busy stealing **ŏ**ranges. (Some people nickname this robber "**or**biting **or**" because he often runs in circles as he looks f**or** m**or**e oranges to steal.)

Report Orvil Or !

absorb	export	glory	orchard	organise	resort	support
assorted	forgiven	inform	orchid	ornament	scornful	thorn
born	fork	import	ordain	orphan	short	torch
border	forlorn	important	order	platform	snort	torch
cord	form	lord	ordinary	pork	sort	transform
corner	forth	normal	organdy	reform	storm	enforce
distort	fortress	north	organic	report(ed)	story	force

Cornelia, Cordelia, Dora, George, Nora, Norman, Victor, Victoria.

> **Picture code each o and ur**

1. In one story Orvil Or has a white horse.
2. The storm on the border ended the next morning.

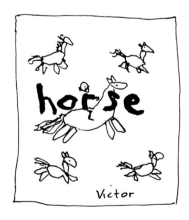

The word oar   Treat **oar** simply as oral information at this point. Words spelt with **oar**, **ore**, **oor** and **our** are listed below.

Or in the Word Orange   Few children notice that **Or**vil **Or** is not saying **or** in the word **ŏ**range. Praise anyone who does. Explain that every **r**obber feels lazy at times and does not bother to steal, see page 144.

Confusions between Two Common Words: house and horse   Help children to notice the **or** pattern in **horse** but *not* in **house**, by making a Spelling Picture of **Or**vil **Or** on a h**or**se in the word **horse**.

Professions   Many end in -**er**, e.g. butch**er**, bak**er**, etc. but many end in -**or** too. One amusing way to learn the -**or** professions is to picture them in think bubbles around a rueful looking **Or**vil **Or**. He is thinking of all the money he could have earned if he had only become a bus conduct**or**, or a doct**or**, a sail**or**, an act**or**, etc. instead of an orange stealer!

Follow Up   Write out and sing the **Orange Stealer's** song, Songbook and Audio Tape 2B.

Orvil Or Never Lets Magic E Stop Him from Stealing Oranges

Orvil **Or** can't aff**or**d to let a Magic **e** send its Magic Sparks over his head and make his stolen **or**ange disappear. So he stops the magic by sh**or**tening the wand with a sc**or**ching blow from his oar.

He stole more oranges down by the shore.

adore	chore	folklore	ignore	seashore	sore	therefore
ashore	core	foreshorten	implore	score	spore	tore
before	deplore	furthermore	pore	shore	store	wherefore
boredom	explore	galore	restore	snore	swore	wore

Picture code each ore

1. He swore that he adored her more than before.
2. The first time he wore the jacket he tore it.

Orvil Or Captures Two Vowels

Whether he captures one vowel or two, it is all the same to **Or**vil **Or**! He just goes on reporting back with his surname '**Or**' as he has always done before. (A low priority story.)

Can we make four doors from these floor boards?

oar	hoarse
oarsman	hoard
board	hoary
coarsened	soaring

poor	outdoors
door	moor
floor	moorhen
indoors	moorland

course	pour
four	your
fourteen	yours
mourn	source

There are too few words in these groups to rate Picture Code Cards, but the pictograms are easily drawn by hand on particular words which give difficulty.

See also page 23 Charts.

Exceptions: our, hour, flour, sour, scour, devour; and words which can sound like **ur**, e.g. armour, favour.

The Three Robber Brothers Called the ER Brothers

We three broth**er**s are the **Er** Broth**er**s.

We take t**ur**ns at saying { **er** **ur**, in many w[or]ds. **ir** }

Of course we each prefer

A different spelling for { **er** **ur**, **ir** }

And while this may seen abs**ur**d
At f**ir**st, or p**ur**poseless, or w[or]se,

We three broth**er**s think we're p**er**fect!
Be al**er**t and obs**er**ve us, we are p**er**fect!

See Letterland Songbook and Audio Tape 2B for the music to these verses. (For boxed words, see page 144.)

Ernest Er, the Elephant Stealer

Meet the first of the vowel-stealing **Er** Broth**er**s. The **Er** Broth**er**s may think they are p**er**fect, but they are really p**er**fectly dreadful. Why? Because they steal so often in words! F**ur**th**er**mo**re** they always quarrel about how to spell their s**ur**name which really makes them trouble-mak**er**s of the f**ir**st ord**er**!

Now look closely at the three **Er** Broth**er**s cards. There is something diff**er**ent about **Er** Broth**er**, **Er**nest **Er**. Have you noticed? His legs are long**er** than eith**er** of his robb**er** broth**er**s. This is why you so often hear him saying "**er**" at the *end* of words. Since he is a fast**er** runn**er** he gets to the end of most words ahead of his oth**er** robb**er** broth**er**s, **Ur**gent **Ur** and **Ir**ving **Ir** (see below).

This broth**er** is a fast**er** runn**er**.

Robber **R**ed runs up to Eddy Elephant · **r̂ed** · but · **Er**nest **Er** steals Eddy Elephant. · **r̂edder**

after	ever	merchant	pattern	refer	silver	universe
alert	expert	modern	perch	remember	sister	verb
another	father	monster	perfect	reserve	sooner	adverb
brother	fern	mother	perform	reserved	stern	verse
confer	however	number	poverty	September	summer	weather
customer	insert	observe	proper	sermon	term	winter
danger	liberty	other	property	shelter	transfer	Germany
dessert	member	passenger	propeller	shepherd	under	

better	colder	harder	redder	softer
bigger	darker	lighter	richer	swifter
blacker	fresher	longer	shorter	thicker
cleaner	greener	quicker	simpler	tighter

and hundreds of other comparative words.

			Surnames with two robberies in them:		
Albert	Gertrude	Percy	Carpenter	Mortimer	Cornford
Alexander	Herbert	Robert	Porter	Archer	Farmer
Bertram	Hester	Rupert	Rutherford	Barber	Gardener
Esther	Jennifer	Veronica	Turner	Barker	Harper
Ferdinand	Oliver	Walter			

Picture code each r and er

1. This robber eats hamburgers for dessert!
2. Can't you be quicker at serving these customers?

Unaccented Syllables with er When there is no emphasis on the **er** syllable it tends to be pronounced unclearly. The children can help themselves with the spelling if they exaggerate the sound of the **er** syllable, so as not to omit the **e**: cam**er**a, diff**er**ent, mis**er**able, sev**er**al, prosp**er**ous.

Ernest Er Twice in a Word. Ernest **Er** is such a fast runner that he can even steal twice in the same word!

caterer	perimeter	wanderer
discoverer	southerner	westerner

Ernest Er Steals a Magic e

When **Er**nest **Er** is feeling especially daring (which is about half the time) he steals a Magic **e**. As he grabs the Magic **e** he runs off so fast that he doesn't even notice that he has left the hat and wand in place. So the Magic Sparks keep on firing away while **Er**nest **Er** says "er!". **Er**nest **Er** thinks he is very clev**er**, but he nev**er** discov**er**s that the Magic Sparks are still getting ov**er**. So he can't be that clev**er**, can he!

Howev**er**, *you* can be clev**er**. If you can't read a word with **Er**nest **Er** in it, check the previous vowel. **Er**nest **Er** may have stolen a Magic **e** and let the sparks get ov**er** to make a Vowel Man appear and say his name.

It is safer to rescue the Magic e later.

accuser	composer	diver	joker	miner	producer	tiger
admirer	computer	driver	later	nicer	ruler	user
baker	consumer	engraver	lifesaver	October	safer	voter
braver	crater	glider	liner	over	skyscraper	whiter
cater	cuter	grocer	maker	paper	sober	wiper
clover	debater	invader	meter	poker	striker	writer

Picture code each Magic e, er and Magic ẽr

1. This Chinese paper is much whiter than the other paper.
2. The invaders jumped over the smaller craters.

Vowels Often Need Protecting from Stolen Magic e's Sparks

Since **Er**nest **Er** often steals a Magic **e**, the vowel sound in the first half of the word often needs to be protected so that it is not replaced by a Vowel Man. Once again a Best Friend must come to the rescue! (See page 82.)

banner	dagger	gutter	mutter	scatter	sputter
better	dimmer	glimmer	otter	suffer	stagger
bitter	dinner	hotter	pepper	summer	stutter
buffer	dipper	kidnapper	planner	supper	thinner
butter	differ	letter	redder	shutter	trapper
clatter	fatter	litter	robber	slipper	trigger
clutter	flatter	madder	rubber	slimmer	twitter
copper	flipper	matter	rugger	sinner	upper
cutter	flutter	manners	runner	soccer	wetter

Picture code each Magic e, each er and Magic er

1. The diver with the flippers was my lifesaver.
2. The driver swerved and missed the gutter.

Follow Up   Collect and use both **er** and Magic **er** words in a piece of creative writing. Sing the **Ernest Er in Person** song, Songbook and Audio Tape 2B.

Urgent Ur, the Umbrella Stealer

Urgent **Ur**'s t**ur**n to steal does not occ**ur** as often as the Elephant Stealer's t**ur**n because **Ur**gent **Ur** is a slower **Er** Broth**er**. As you can see his legs are not as long as those of fast**er Er**nest **Er**. On top of that the silly fellow will wear those thick boots of c**ur**ly f**ur**, so he can't exactly sp**ur**t along, can he? As a result **Ur**gent **Ur** is seldom seen at the ends of words, only from time to time inside words and hardly ever at the beginning of a word.

Each Thursday he returns.

burglar	curtain	further	purple	surface	turn
burn	disturb	hurt	purpose	surprise	turnip
burst	fur	injure	purse	survive	turtle
church	furnish	murder	return	Thursday	urge
curl	furry	nurse	Saturday	turkey	urgent

(See also words with -**ture**, page 147.)

Picture code each u, r and ur

1. Quick, run and turn off the burner.
2. Do not disturb Ursula in church.

Use Purple as a Spelling Aid   Urgent **Ur**'s favourite colour is . . . .? Purple, of course! You may like to suggest some creative writing where everything **Ur**gent **Ur** steals turns purple at his touch. Or ask the children, how many **ur** words can they draw in one picture? A nurse eating turnips? A burglar stealing a purple turkey near a church? A nurse with curly hair feeding yogurt to a turtle? Or a surgeon surrounded by purple curtains and purple furniture? The more unlikely the better, with each purple object labelled, written with a purple felt pen. (See also the **Ur** song, Letterland Songbook and Audio Tape 2B.)

Exceptions: most words ending in -**our**.

Irving Ir, the Ink Stealer

Irving **Ir** is the third rober brother. He turns up in far fewer words than either of the other two brothers. This is because he thinks most **i**nk is not worth stealing. The kind of **i**nk Irving **Ir** really wants to steal is gold **i**nk or silver **i**nk. But this is very difficult to find. (You sometimes see it on book covers.) So he has to make do with blue **i**nk.

You might think that Irving Ir would check that the lid was tightly shut on any **i**nk bottle he decided to steal. But no, the silly fellow never checks! This is why he always wears a dirty shirt. Virtually every shirt he owns has **i**nk stains on it! (The 'Irving Ir in Person' song on Audio Tape 2B supports both the **ir** sound and words spelt with **ir**.)

This is not his first dirty shirt.

bird	fir	irk	shirt	stir	thirty-first	whir
birch	firm	irksome	skirmish	stirring	thirty-third	whirring
birthday	confirm	mirth	skirt	swirl	thirst	circle
chirp	first	quirk	smirk	third	thirsty	circus
dirt	flirt	sir	squirm	thirteen	twirl	virgin
dirty	girl	shirk	squirt	thirty	whirl	virtue

> **Picture code each i, r and ir**

1. Climbing firs and birch trees can be risky.
2. First Shirley will give the thirsty birds a drink.

Which Brother? Er? Ur? or Ir?   (The Er Brother's Quarrel). Absurd or perfect though it may be (depending how you look at it) the three **Er** brothers have never agreed on the correct spelling of their surname.

Ernest **Er** says it should be **er** to match *his* first name. **Ur**gent **Ur** says it should be **ur** to match *his* first name. And Irving **Ir** says it should be **ir** to match *his* first name. Believe it or not they are still quarrelling. As a result we can never be sure which **Er** Brother we hear in a word. It is all those wretched **Er** Brothers' fault for quarrelling about their surname in the first place. The quickest way to get the better of them, however, is to make up and collect sentences with only one brother in them.

Deduction Strategy   For especially weak spellers limit your focus on **ur** and **ir** to the few words the children will need most. (The five most common **ir** words are bird, birthday, first, girl and third.) Each child should devise as short a sentence as possible selecting the **ir** words which *they* think they will need most often. Once they have learnt all the common **ir** and **ur** words, they can, if in doubt, feel saf**er** by opting for **er**, rath**er** than eith**er** of the oth**er** robb**er** broth**er**s!

Irving Ir Is Overpowered by Magic e

Irving **Ir** could easily break the wand and stop the Magic Sparks from getting his stolen letter out of his sack. All the other **robber**s do! But the truth is, **Ir**ving **Ir** is frightened of the Magic Sparks. So he just ducks and lets the sparks jump over him, making his **i**nk disappear and Mr **I** appear instead. So when you see the Ink Stealer in a word, and are about to say "**ir**", think again if you see a Magic **e** next in the word. **Ir**ving is the only **r**obber who is afraid of Magic **e**'s.

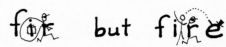

admire	enquire	inspire	perspire	satire	sire
dire	fire	inquire	require	sapphire	spire
empire	hire	mire	retire	shire	vampire

Note. There are too few common **ire** words for a Picture Code Card, but it is shown on a **r**obber Flap Chart.

Don't Let Them Get Away With It! If a child reads a list such as this one, correctly up to h**ur**t but then starts to sound out **hurt** with "h**ŭ** . . .", interrupt him to say playfully, "Help, help! The Umbrella Stealer seems to be able to steal that **u**mbrella right in front of your nose without you noticing him! I am sure you are a better detective than that. This page is full of words with robberies in them, all done by the **Er** Broth**er**s who all say . . . .? You caught the Ink Stealer saying **ir** in f**ir**st and b**ir**d. What about the Umbrella Stealer? What does he say? Isn't he an **Er** Broth**er** too? You draw on his head and legs. Put his stolen letter in his sack to show you have caught him in the act. Now try reading that word again." (While not all children want to learn to read, most children are keen to catch **r**obbers!)

Catch him!

the first bird
his finger hurts
dog's curly fur
bigger girl
fresher ferns

Collect Words with Several Robbers in Them The best detectives can identify any **r**obber instantly, even when there are several **r**obbers all running along in one word.

conjurer transformer dirtier
gardener lecturer

adventurer	carpenter	explorer	lecturer	performer	starter
astronomer	conjurer	farmer	murderer	purchaser	surgery
barber	curler	former	murkier	pursuer	surrender

Ideally, do not just give children copies of this list: help them to make their own collections by allowing time to skim through classroom books. This skimming is good practice towards more general information-searching skills.

More About Kicking King

Only 36 high-usage words begin with **k**. Nearly half begin with silent **kn**, which is very confusing since they sound as though they began with **n**. The most important **kn** words to read and spell correctly are **known**, **knows** and **knew** (easily confused with **no**, **nose**, and **new**). Who is to blame for all these confusions? Naughty Nick, of course! He can also be blamed in -**nk** words for typical errors such as thinck, thingk, thingck (**think**), thanck, thack (**thank**), dongkey, docky (**donkey**). The best time to tell either of the following stories is when a mistake crops up. Omit the -**nk** story altogether if no child needs it. The -**rk** story will help to clear up typical errors such as **darck** and **worck**. Again omit it if no child needs it. The brief section on **lk** gives attention to the few words which end in -**lk**.

The Kicking King Never Kicks Nick

The Kicking King loves kicking but he never kicks when he is next to Nick in a word. Why not? Because Naughty Nick has a **kn**ack of getting in his way. So then the King cannot kick. Instead he frowns angrily and points silently at Nick for being such a **n**uisance.

We know that Nick has a knack of being a nuisance.

knee	knelt	knick-knack	knight	knives	knock	know	knows
kneel	knew	knock-kneed	knit	knob	knot	knowledge	known

Picture code each n, k and kn

1. The unknown knight killed the dragon with a knife.
2. No one knew the wicked knave who stole the knapsack.

Nick Scares Clever Cat Away from the Kicking King

Clever Cat and the King finish many short words together but not when Naughty Nick is behind the King's back. Then the naughty fellow, instead of saying "**nnn** . . ." as usual, makes an "**ng**" sound. Clever Cat is startled by his sudden change of tune so, when Nick is around, she runs away instead of staying to watch the King kick.

" No, thanks," she thinks.

bank	conker	donkey	hunk	pink	sank	stink	think
bonk	chink	drink	ink	plank	sunk	stank	trinket
bunk	chunk	drank	junk	plonk	shrink	swank	trunk
blink	clink	drunk	kink	punk	shrank	tinker	twinkle
blanket	crank	hanky	monkey	rank	slink	tank	yank

118

1. Nick has a trunk full of clocks and bits of junk.
2. The blanket with checks on it has shrunk.

Any Robber will Scare the Cat Away from Kicking King

Clever Cat and the Kicking King finish up many short words together but not when there's a **r**obber near by. Whether it's **Ar**thur **Ar**, or any other **r**obber, you can be sure Clever Cat will get away fast because she is frightened of **r**obbers.

I see a fox lurking in the dark.

ark	hark	postmark	jerk	smirk	pitchfork	clockwork	lurk
bark	lark	remark	perk	quirk	pork	network	Turk
dark	mark	spark	irk	cork	stork	patchwork	turkey
embark	park	stark	shirk	fork	work	York	murky

**Picture code
ck and rk**

1. The pitchfork struck a spark on the rock.
2. The card is postmarked York.

Word Ending in lk

No Pictogram is provided for these few words, but we know that the Lamp Lady loves to **walk** and **talk** with the King. What a pity there are only about six words where she has a chance to shine right beside her sovereign!

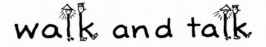

walk and talk

walk	talk	chalk	milk	silk	folk

What Happens To Clever Cat Beside E, I and Y

Many children learn that **c** sometimes sounds like **s**. This is important to know. But they also need to know exactly *when* to read **c** as "sss . . .". In fact the 'soft' sound is entirely predictable. The *next letter* in the word provides the clue. Either teach **ce**, **ci** and **cy** together or delay your introduction of **ci** and **cy** until

later, according to your children's needs. The children confirm the **e**'s signalling power by drawing the top hat on the **e**, and going right between the **c** and **e**, to 'fire off' the blue sparks straight at the open side of the **c**. On the Flap Chart colour the hollow **c**'s, **e**, **i** and **y** all light blue. Let the children also overwrite the

ce, **ci**, **cy** patterns in blue, when they picture code soft **c** words. Play-acting the story only takes a minute; time which will be well spent in making the Blue Magic concept indelible. Blue Magic has only two targets: **c** and **g**. (For the **ge, gi,** and **gy** stories see page 125).

Clever Cat Turns into a Hissing Snake Beside E

Cats and **s**nakes do not usually like each other. But the Hairy Hat Man has both a **c**at and a **s**nake for pets (see **ch** and **sh**). Mr E thinks it's a pity that these two pets cannot enjoy each other's company and he has a bright idea. "It's **eee**asy," he says. "If I turn Clever Cat into a **s**nake they *can* enjoy playing together!" So he makes a new kind of silent Magic **e**.

This **e**'s sparks are *blue*. They are not powerful enough to jump back over one letter to make a Vowel Man appear, like the jumping *yellow* sparks. The blue sparks are only strong enough to change Clever Cat into a snake if she is *right next* to Blue Magic **e**. Then hey presto! She becomes a little snake and Clever Cat and Sammy Snake can have a fine time both hissing in words - until the magic wears off. Then Clever Cat becomes a **c**at again and goes back to making her little '**c**..' sound in words, as usual.

In this sentence we both hiss nicely.

ace*	choice	face*	lace*	pace*	princess	since
advice*	dance	fence	lice*	pence	race*	slice*
balance	dice*	force	mince	place*	rice*	place
cancel	disgrace*	glance	nice*	price*	romance	trace*
central	entrance	grace*	office	prince	scent	twice*
chance	except	ice*	once	scene*	sentence	voice

Alice, Celia, Cedric, Clarence, Florence, Frances, Grace*, Janice, Jocelyn, Joyce, Laurence, Maurice, Prudence, Terence, Vincent.

* The starred words indicate **e**'s which shoot both *blue* sparks and *yellow* sparks. Congratulate any child who spots this double function and show everyone the Extra Electric **e** side of your Blue Magic **e** Picture Code Card.

absence	celery	certain	deceitful	finance	piece
ambulance	cement	certificate	difference	glance	peace
admittance	centipede	choice	embrace	grocer	percent
allowance	censor	conceal	evidence	groceries	process
ancestor	cereal	conceited	excellence	hence	recent
cancer	century	concern	exception	importance	surface
cease	ceremony	convince	existence	niece	terrace

Exceptions   Blue Magic power failures are rare. S**ce**ptical is one such. Can you find any others?

Decide: -ence/-ance or -ense/-anse?   Clever Cat appears in several hundred -en**ce** and -an**ce** words. By contrast Sammy Snake only finishes about twelve. They include exp**anse**, imm**ense**, s**ense** and the verb lic**ense** (but not the noun lic**ence**).

Can you spot the sparks once or twice?

> **Picture code each c, s and ce**

1. Colin wrote a sentence about a race in a spaceship.
2. My advice is to cancel the dance at the palace.

Blue Magic Only Works from One Side of Clever Cat

collect
necklace

If you see an **e** on the closed side of Clever Cat's face it will not be a blue Magic **e**. Blue Magic **e**'s aim only at her open side, shooting towards what becomes her stomach.

What Happens to Clever Cat's Cousin Carol

accept
eccentric

Blue magic can neither jump nor reach back over two letters, so when Clever Cat and her country cousin Clever Cat are side by side, *only* Clever Carol next to Blue Magic **e** is turned into a hissing snake.

> **Picture code each hard cc and cce**

1. He is not accustomed to accepting gifts.
2. The job was successfully accomplished.

One Exception: A 'power failure' in the word so**cc**er, so neither cat is turned into a hissing little snake.

soccer

Clever Cat Turns into a Hissing Snake before i

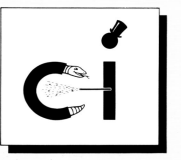

Clever Cat finds it very exciting to hiss like Sammy, but Mr E is a very busy man. So he looks for another letter he can trust to shoot Blue Magic for him, and chooses **i**. Mr E just leaves his top hat on the **i**-dot and a spare wand to shoot the blue sparks. Hey presto! Once again Clever Cat becomes a **s**nake so she can hiss just like Sammy.

Come to the exciting circus in the city.

acid	circle	city	concise	incident	rancid
accident	circulation	civil	decide	medicine	scientist
calcium	cigar	civilization	decimal	merciful	penicillin
capacity	circus	council	electricity	pencil	society
cigarette	citizen	criticise	fascinate	precise	specific

Cecilia, Cinderella, Francis, Felicity, Lucille, Lucinda, Millicent, Priscilla, Sicily, Pacific.

Exception: when **ci** sounds like **sh** (see page 152).

> **Picture code each s, c and ci**

1. He described a small accident in the city.
2. Eric decided to come with us to the circus.   accident

Blue Magic Sparks Shoot From Magic ing

dance
dancing

Because **ing** is a magic ending it can shoot *blue* magic sparks just as easily as it shoots jumping, yellow magic sparks. So when a word ends with a Blue Magic E it can easily be replaced by an equally Blue Magic **ing**! (More examples in the list of **ce** words.)

Several common words end in Extra Electric **e**'s where both kinds of magic are sparking away at the same time. When **ing** replaces a Blue Magic **e** then **ing** becomes an 'extra electric ending'!

face
fac....
facing

facing   racing   icing   producing

pacing	spacing	slicing	producing
placing	tracing	spicing	replacing

> **Picture code each c, Magic e and Magic ing**

1. We are reducing our rate for producing rice.
2. Slicing through this icing is difficult.

Note.   The only times that the letter **i** becomes magic are in Magic **ing**, and in **ci** and **gi**. At no other times does Mr E lend his magic power to **i** (yellow sparks or blue).

<table>
<tr><td>

Picture code each s c, ce and ci

</td><td>

1. He has certainly decided he must get a licence.
2. He received a Swimming Certificate from the City Club.

</td></tr>
</table>

Blue Magic on Signs   Many towns have a fine example of both kinds of soft **c** on their CITY CENTRE signs. Scout around for other good ones, paint and code them. After the **cy** pictogram below add further examples.

Both ce and ci in the Same Word   At least six words contain both **ce** and **ci**. Who can find more?

science,   coincidence
circumstance,   circumference
Cecil   Cecilia

Clever Cat Turns into a Hissing Snake before Y

The only other letter which Mr E trusts to handle blue magic for him is the Yo-yo Man. So the only other time Clever Cat has a chance to be transformed into a hissing snake is when she is next to the Yo-yo Man. Then once again she can hiss just like Sammy Snake.

I fancy it is
the safest policy.

agency	cygnet	decency	encyclopedia	pharmacy	saucy	tendency
bicycle	cylinder	delicacy	fancy	policy	scythe	urgency
currency	cymbal	democracy	frequency	pregnancy	spicy	vacancy
cycle	cynical	diplomacy	juicy	privacy	secrecy	
cyclone	cypress	emergency	lacy	racy	supremacy	

Cyprus   Cynthia   Cyril   Lucy   Nancy   Percy

<table>
<tr><td>

Picture code each cy

</td><td>

1. This juicy, spicy fruit comes from Cyprus.
2. Where is Lucy's pet cygnet?

</td></tr>
</table>

Play Act Soft c : ce/ci/cy

Prepare a cat headband, a wand, a large card with **c** (cat coding) on one side and **c** (snake coding) on the other, and an equally large Blue Magic **e**.

The **c**-child stands saying "**c** . . . **c** . . . **c** . . ." as the **e**-child approaches on tip-toe and silently 'fires' his Blue Sparks straight at her. The **c**-child swiftly pivots around, turning her card to the **s**nake side while her hands are out of sight. As she completes the pivot she throws off her cat headband and starts hissing loudly. Use the same routine for **ci** and **cy**. Later have six children make additional props and act out **ce**, **ci** and **cy** simultaneously.

Follow Up Exercise: Cat or Snake?

Cat? or Snake?

✓ ~~c~~res~~c~~ent
ancestor
conceal
scent
excellence
process
cement
convince

Choose several words which are outside the children's sight vocabulary. Write them large on the board or on paper. Explain that this time you do *not* want anyone to try to read the words, but only to picture code them.

"Cat? or Snake?", you ask at each **c**. They should spot each **ce**, **ci** or **cy** sequence, answer "Cat" or "Snake" and use a light blue felt pen to overwrite both letters, add top hat, wand and sparks. Then let them go back and work out the words, now confident that they know exactly how to pronounce each **c**. Later they can try the same group of words *without* picture coding support. It only takes a few exer**ci**ses like this to make most children able to predi**c**t every hard or soft **c** in virtually any word.

Ginger, the Gentle Gymnast

Golden Girl, Golden Granny and now Gentle Ginger: why three Letterland characters for **g**? Golden Girl and Golden Granny (also known as Go Go Grannie) both symbolise the hard **g** sound. Both are needed so that words like **egg** and bi**gg**est can be shown clearly as having two hard **g**'s.

The completely different sound made by soft **g** calls for a new Letterland heroine, Gentle Ginger the Gymnast. She is just as athletic as Jumping Jim whose sound is identical to hers. The only difference is that she is far less shy. In fact she loves being watched as she practises her gymnastic tricks in words. This is why she turns up in far more words than Jumping Jim. The soft **g** sound which **G**entle **G**inger, the **G**ymnast symbolises can be heard four times in her name. The signal that tells us when she will appear and make her sound is the next letter: when it is an **e**, **i** or **y**. (Strictly, the second **g** in bi**gg**est should be soft, as in sug**g**est, but it is an exception).

Fold **gi** and **gy** out of sight on the **g** Flap Chart until relevant.

Gentle Ginger, the Gymnast Says "g . . ." Before E.

Golden Girl always says that her Granny is her best friend (see page 51). But she has a special friend at school, too. She is **Ge**ntle **Gi**nger, the **Gy**mnast. Golden Girl admires **Ge**ntle **Gi**nger greatly because **Gi**nger is so good at **gy**mnastics. Somersaults, cartwheels, balancing acts – you name it. She can do it! Golden Girl thinks everyone should notice **Ge**ntle **Gi**nger's **gy**mnastic tricks in words. So she asks Mr E if he could use some of his new Blue Magic **e**'s to light her up with sparkling blue light as she does her somersaults. "**Eee**asily!" cries Mr E, and so he does.

Gentle **Gi**nger is so pleased to be in the limelight that she does her very best somersaults every time she is next to a Blue Magic **e**. She also starts to say her name like this, **ge** . . . for '**Ge**ntle **Gi**nger'. She is practising for the day when she will announce herself in a big gymnastic competition.

Ginger's somersaults are gorgeous.

age	agent	emerge	germs	orange	strange
cage	angel	energetic	ginger	outrageous	suggest
enrage	change	exaggerate	gorge	passenger	surge
huge	charge	fringe	hinge	pigeon	surgeon
page	courageous	gems	indulge	plunge	tangerine
rage	danger	genie	large	range	twinge
refuge	detergent	genius	legend	refugee	urge
stage	digest	generous	messenger	revenge	vegetables
wage(s)	dungeon	gentlemen	midget	sponge	verge

Angela, Bridget, Genevieve, George, Gerald, Geraldine, Nigel, Roger
Argentina, Germany

```
┌─────────────────────┐
│ Picture code        │
│ each g and ge       ├───
└─────────────────────┘
```

1. Can you get Roger to bring us a large hinge?
2. That stranger needs help urgently.

Hard or Soft? Usually an **e** after **cc** or **gg** will only make the neighbouring **c** or **g** soft (e.g. suc**ce**ss, sug**ge**st). While this is a reliable generalization for almost all words with **cc** it does not always hold for **gg**, e.g. two hard **g**'s in bi**gg**er but two soft **g**'s in exa**gge**rate.

The exceptions include some but not all words with **gg**, e.g. bi**gg**est, da**gg**er, tri**gg**er, ru**gg**er and words with **ng** or **gg** plus **ed**, e.g. lon**g**ed, wa**gg**ed. Single **g** exceptions include fin**g**er, **g**et, **g**eese, **G**ertrude, tar**g**et, ti**g**er, to**g**ether. Can your class discover any more?

Silent Duck Beside Gentle Ginger

Normally when you see Dippy Duck in a word you will hear her making her usual little '**d** . . .' sound. But not when the next letters are Gentle Ginger and a blue Magic **e**! Then she is too dazzled by Gentle Ginger's gymnastics to speak!

Let's give her a badge.

-adge	-edge	-idge	-idge	-odge	-udge
badge	edge	abridge	midge	dislodge	budge
badger	hedge	bridge	midget	dodge	fudge
cadge	knowledge	cartridge	partridge	lodge	judge
gadget	sledge	fridge	porridge	stodge	smudge

Sound Alikes: -idge and -age

There are only nine words which end in **i-d-g-e**. They all contain the word **ridge**, except for **midge** and **midget**: ab**ridge**, b**ridge**, cart**ridge**, f**ridge**, part**ridge**, por**ridge**, **ridge**, m**idge**, m**idge**t.

But there are many **a-g-e** words. Some **a-g-e** and all **i-d-g-e** words are pronounced "ige". Since **bridge** is the only frequently used "ige" word ending in **-idge**, a rough generalisation for all other "ige" words is: unless the word is b**ridge**, spell it **a-g-e**.

acreage	courage	image	package	shrinkage
advantage	disadvantage	language	percentage	storage
average	drainage	leakage	postage	usage
bandage	encourage	manage	ravage	vicarage
beverage	haulage	marriage	savage	vintage
bondage	heritage	mileage	salvage	voltage
coinage	homage	mortgage	shortage	voyage

(The only English word actually spelt as it sounds: vest**ige**)

Double Consonants Strangely, in the next seven words the vowels before **-age** words need protecting. Learn them in these two sentences:

I saw his lu**gg**age in the Ba**gg**age Room pa**ss**age, so I left him this me**ss**age. Come and eat ca**bb**age at our co**tt**age in the vi**ll**age.

Gentle Ginger, the Gymnast Says "G . . ." for Ginger before I

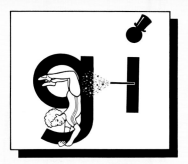

When Mr E is too busy elsewhere to shoot Blue Magic Sparks to light up Gentle **Gi**nger the Gymnast, he generously gives the job to **i**. So the blue sparks shoot straight from **i** to **Gi**nger to light her up. Once again Gentle **Gi**nger is so pleased that she starts to say her name, '**gi** . . .' for **Gi**nger.

See Ginger in blue Magic light.

giant	gipsy	biologist	frigid	logical	original	religion
gigantic	giraffe	engine	geologist	magic	regiment	surgical
gin	gist	engineer	imagine	margin	region	tragic
ginger	agitate	fragile	logic	origin	register	Virginia

aging	bulging	judging	urging
arranging	engaging	raging	waging

Also words listed under **ge** which drop **e** before **ing**.

Exceptions be**g**in, be**g**inning, **g**ift, **g**ive, **g**iving, **g**irl, **g**iggle, be**gg**ing.

> **Picture Code each g and gi**

1. Do giraffes live in this grassy region?
2. The original copy is good, but fragile.

Gentle Ginger, the Gymnast Says "G . . ." for Ginger before Y

In some words Mr E generously gives the Yo-yo Man some of his Blue Magic too. The Yo-yo Man is pleased to do the job of lighting up Ginger's '**gy**rations' for him. Then Ginger smiles engagingly and says "**gy** . ." for **gy**mnast.

I have spongy gym shoes.

allergy	edgy	gym	mangy	spongy
analogy	Egypt	gymkhana	orgy	stodgy
biology	elegy	gymnastics	prodigy	strategy
clergy	energy	ideology	pudgy	zoology

> **Picture code each g and gy**

1. Goodness, such energy for all those gymnastics!
2. My big pony was feeling edgy at the gymkhana.

The Wicked Water Witch at Work in Words

The letter **w** (like **r**) affects the sound of any vowel to its left. So we have words like h**ow**l and b**ow**l, n**ew** and s**aw**. Even worse, **w** often causes a change in a vowel to its right, as in **wa**s, **wa**ter, **wo**rd and **wo**man.

So **w** is a very troublesome letter for all newcomers to reading and spelling. In Letterland terms, **w** is the home of the Wicked Water Witch. She loves confusing everyone. If she had her way she would stop all children from becoming good readers and good spellers. It is up to them to outwit her by learning exactly what happens when she appears in words!

This Witch is, of course, only a little 'paper witch' and no real threat. In fact, she can be a welcome scapegoat for mistakes in spelling. Besides, she is also foolish and clumsy, so the children can enjoy showing her up in words. Do not be surprised if you are soon asked, "When can we have another story about the Wicked Water Witch?" Children like to match their wits against hers. This section covers **ow**, **ōw** and **ou**. For **aw**, **au** and **ew** stories see pages 138 and 107.

When she Tries to Get the Orange the Witch Howls "ow."

The Wicked Water Witch loves the big, round, ripe **o**ranges which Mr O imports from over the ocean. She knows these **o**ranges do not belong to her, but that does not stop her from wanting them! Every time she finds herself next to an **o**range in a word she tries a wicked spell to get it out.

Luckily for the **o**range, the Witch is clumsy and foolish as well. When her spell doesn't work (and it never seems to), she gets so angry that she tries to break open the **o** with her broomstick. But she always falls and bumps her chin instead.

That is why, in lots of words where you see these two letters, all you can hear is the Wicked Water Witch h**ow**ling "**ow**!".

The Vowel Men said that the witch howled, "ōw"!

allow	crowd	eyebrow	gown	howl	prowl	somehow
brown	down	flower	growl	owl	renowned	towel
clown	drown	fowl	how	powder	rowdy	town
cowslip	drowsy	frown	however	power	shower	vowel

Picture code each ow ⟩

1. His eyebrows look black when he frowns.
2. My dog howls at the owls.

128

When Mr O Surprises the Witch They Both Cry "O".

Mr O knows that the Witch is after his **o**ranges. "Oh no you don't!" says Mr O. Although he is very old, he manages to stop her by crying out his name "O" to show that this **o**range belongs to him.

At the very same moment she cries out, "Oh!" in surprise. Can you hear them both crying "ō!" in all the words listed bel**ow**?

The old fellow shows her who owns the oranges.

aglow	bow	follow	hallowed	overthrow	show	thrown
arrow	bowler	flow	know	owed	shown	tow
below	bowling	flown	known	owes	slow	unknown
bellow	bungalow	glow	low	owner	sorrow	widow
blow	crow	grow	mellow	pillow	snow	willow
blown	elbow	grown	mow	shadow	sparrow	window
borrow	fellow	hedgerow	narrow	shallow	throw	yellow

Picture code each w and ow

1. The snow is blowing in the window.
2. Wendy's pet sparrow is slowly growing.

Picture code both sounds of ow

1. how low
2. slowly now
3. below the town
4. owl in the snow
5. yellow cowslip
6. follow the crowd
7. growing flowers
8. throw down
9. brown shadow
10. power mower
11. show how
12. rowdy crowd

129

The Witch knows Mr O will stop her from trying to get his **o**ranges whenever he can. So she decides to hide inside a different letter where not even old Mr O would expect to find her. Can you think of another letter which could hold water? The Witch can! The **u**mbrella letter! Her problem is that Uppy Umbrella is usually there protecting it from getting wet. So what does the Wicked Water Witch do?

She uses her broomstick like a hose, shooting water at poor Uppy Umbrella. The water lifts Uppy up and sends her flying. While she is gone the Wicked Witch quickly fills her tub-shaped letter full of water, dives down under and tries an **u**nderwater-spell to get the **o**range **ou**t. Silly witch! Her **u**nderwater-spells do not work properly either! Again she tries to break into the **o** with her broomstick!

Can you imagine trying to hit anything hard when you are **u**nderwater? It is not surprising that every time she tries she just fl**ou**nders, bumps her chin again and sh**ou**ts "**ou**!" The chances are that the only s**ou**nd you will hear is the Witch sh**ou**ting "**ou**!"

We found her shouting "OU" very loudly.

about	couch	doubt	house	noun	pound	sound	surround
account	count	flour	loud	ouch	pounce	sour	thousand
around	countess	found	mound	ounce	proud	south	trousers
blouse	county	ground	mouse	our	round	spout	trout
bounce	crouch	hour	mount	out	shout	sprout	vouch
cloud	devour	hound	mouth	pouch	snout	stout	voucher

One thousand pounds.

Picture code
each o, u and ou

1. Our house is just south of a round about.
2. The pig had mud on his snout and mouth.

Candle Magic

Since **l** and **e** together are usually pronounced '**le**..' as in le**tter**, children are often surprised that the same two letters make an "ul" sound at the end of words. It is important for children who spell by ear to identify this final "ul" sound if they are to avoid endlessly spelling it **-ul**

or **-el**. Both will be incorrect far more often than **-le** since over 270 common words end in **-le**. The second point about **-le** is exciting: it is a Magic Ending! Revise the fact that Magic **e**'s at the end of a word make **a**pples (etc.) vanish and Vowel Men appear to say their names instead (page 68–74).

Letterland's Magic Endings **ed**, **en**, **est** and **ing** also behave exactly like Magic **e**'s (page 76–81). This new magic Ending is a litt**le** bit different. It is called 'Candle Magic' (stress the **le** sound) to point up that difference.

Candle Magic with e for a Handle

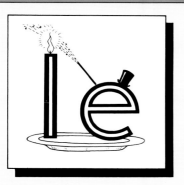

Cand**le** Magic works like this. First of all yellow sparks shoot up from Magic **e** and transform Lucy, the Lamp Lady into a big, magic cand**le** – quite a trick in itself! The **e**'s Magic Sparks then light the cand**le** so that the cand**le** has more magic than Magic **e** itself. The **e** simply becomes the cand**le**stick hand**le**. *If* there is a single vowel within firing range the magic cand**le** will shoot sparks up and over *one* letter, just as yellow, jumping sparks usually do, but *these* sparks always jump back from the *top* of the cand**le** instead of from the Magic **e**. That is why Letterland people call this ending 'Cand**le** Magic'. (Follow up with Songbook and Audio Tape 2B.)

The candle is in the middle of the table.

able	cable	idle	ogle	stable
bible	cradle	isle	rifle	stifle
bridle	disciple	ladle	scruple	table
bugle	fable	noble	sidle	trifle

bridle

map but maple   is but isle

bib but bible   cab but cable

Picture code each vowel and le	1. The lad playing the bugle is able but idle.
	2. The Bible tells us of Jesus and his disciples.

Best Friend to the Rescue

The second **t** in **little** is a useful example of a vowel being rescued from Can**dle** Magic's sparks. Now at last the children can see why they always need two **t**'s in litt**le**. The second **t** stops the word from becoming "litle" (as in **title**). Encourage them to pronounce any mistakes just as their mis-spelling indicates. Amusing examples: winning a "bātle", dropping a "bōtle" in the "mīdle" of the road, blowing on a "bŭggle", etc. Enjoy and learn from the mistakes.

The trick is to listen to the vowel sound before -**le**, e.g. "pǎd . . .le". If they *don't* want Candle Magic to make a Vowel Man appear, they should call a Best Friend to protect the **a**pple. Who wants to **pādle** a canoe? Support your point by play-acting the Rescue song, Letterland Songbook and Audio Tape 2B.

apple	cripple	nobble	muddle	pebble	scribble	smuggle
babble	cuddle	huddle	muzzle	puzzle	scuffle	squabble
battle	dazzle	juggle	nettle	quibble	scuttle	throttle
bottle	dribble	kettle	nibble	rattle	settle	tussle
brittle	drizzle	little	nuzzle	riddle	shuffle	wiggle
bubble	giggle	meddle	paddle	ripple	snuffle	wobble
cattle	guzzle	middle	puddle	ruffle	sizzle	wriggle

> **Picture code each l and le**

1. Let's blow bubbles into a bottle.
2. The title of that blue book puzzles me.

Practise Handling Candle Magic Sparks

 ✓

 ✗

Picture coding allows children to check their own decisions whether or not to call in a 'Best Friend' to protect a short vowel. Dictate a few words, e.g. **rifle**, **saddle**, **fable** and **giggle**. When they have finished writing, say "Light your can**dle**, shoot your Magic Sparks from the top of the can**dle** and decide whether or not you have hand**led** the Can**dle** Magic correctly. Have you written **rifle** or **riffle**?" and so on. Like checking their own sums they discover whether the word 'adds up' correctly or not.

Other Ways of Protecting Vowels

Two Different Consonants Do not try to protect a vowel if it is two letters away from the can**dle**. It is already too far away to need protection. The can**dle** won't waste its sparks.

an**gle**	exa**mple**	ga**mble**	ki**ndle**	swi**ndle**
ca**ndle**	fu**mble**	ju**ngle**	si**mple**	te**mple**

Protection from ck Since Letterland has only one King you will never see **kk**. If you hear a 'k' sound before -**le** call in the **c**at and the **k**ing to protect your vowel from the Can**dle** Magic's sparks.

buckle	freckle	knuckle	prickle	tickle
crackle	heckle	pickle	tackle	trickle

Confusion Between le and ly

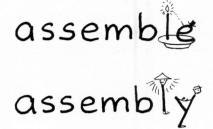

Inexperienced spellers often expect that **le** ("ul") can be used to spell **ly** ("lee"). Remind them that it is no use trying to spell a final "e" sound with **e** because the moment they set it at the end of a word it will automatically become a silent **e**, in this case a silent **e** hand**le**! Useful examples for comparing -**le** and -**ly** are:

assemble	bubble	pebble
assembly	bubbly	pebbly

Compare les and less

Virtually all words which end in -**les** are pronounced as in cand**les**. Let the children picture code words with **less** in the same lesson to 'see' the contrast in sound for themselves, e.g. whist**les**, wit**less**; wrest**les**, rest**less**.

The 'UL' Sound: le? al? el?

-al

Not all words which contain a final '**ul**' sound are spelt with **le**. For words ending in **ful** see page 101. The remaining alternatives are **al** and **el**. Many of the words ending in **al** are predictable, once the children learn that **al** means "to do with". There is no Picture Code Card for the **al** suffix.

accidental	experimental	magical	chemical	logical	reversal
biblical	factual	musical	classical	national	sensational
comical	historical	personal	emotional	natural	structural
continental	horizontal	postal	external	oriental	survival
critical	hospital	rental	liberal	removal	universal

-el

There are roughly 18 common words ending in **el** sounding like '**ul**'. Learn them one at a time as needed, or in small groups.

angel	camel	chapel	label	marvel	parcel	satchel	squirrel	travel
barrel	channel	kennel	model	novel	quarrel	shovel	towel	tunnel

For words ending in **ible** or **able** see page 155.

Flap Charts: -le The -**le** pictogram appears on two Flap Charts. The first one makes comparison easy between **le** and **ly**. The second Flap Chart shows it with -**al** and -**el**.

Sometimes Magic

There is no way to predict exactly when **y** will 'shoot the Magic Sparks' (make the preceding vowel say its name). It is worth knowing, however, that this happens quite often. The evidence lies not only in words like **bony, tiny,** etc. but also in the sizeable number of words where double consonants are required to keep the preceding vowel short, as in **bonny, tinny,** etc.

When summing up the Magic Endings, **er** needs to be included. You may like to add a ½ figure to the **y, er** Display Chart (see page 22) to show that these endings are only Magic roughly half of the time.

The Yo-yo Man Can Shoot Magic for Mr E

The Yo-yo Man is very glad to work for Mr E, saying "**ē**" for him at the ends of many words. But he especially proud when the magician asks him to shoot Magic Sparks, as well as saying Mr E's name for him. This means *he* can play the Naming Game with the Vowel Men! In fact he manages the Magic Sparks so well that roughly half of the times he appears in short words for Mr E, he shoots the sparks for Mr E.

baby   tiny   stony   duty

baby	lazy	shady	icy	slimy	bony	pony	duly	ruby
crazy	navy	shaky	ivy	tidy	cosy	stony	duty	Judy
lady	scaly	wavy	shiny	tiny				

In many of these short words (usually two-syllable words only) you will need to call in a Best Friend to protect the vowel from the Magic Sparks.

Daddy   silly   hobby   funny

Mummy	Jimmy	marry	penny	witty	poppy	dummy	muggy
Daddy	Tommy	shabby	giddy	foggy	soggy	fluffy	nutty
Betty	Willy	berry	jiffy	floppy	sorry	funny	puffy
Dotty	baggy	cherry	dizzy	jolly	sloppy	fuzzy	puppy
Jenny	carry	jelly	silly	groggy	spotty	hurry	sunny
Penny	flabby	merry	frizzy	hobby	bunny	muddy	stuffy

Picture code each vowel and y

1. Amy is a jolly lady with a rosy face.
2. Hurry up and tidy Mummy's kitchen.
3. At home it is sunny or shady, or foggy and muddy at times.

Reminder Watch out, too, for **er**. It becomes a Magic Ending roughly half of the time (see pages 114–115). The vowel within reach of its Magic Sparks may also need protection.

The Yo-yo Man's Changing Hut

Children are slow to learn when they can see no reason for a shift in spelling patterns. So they will add **s** not only to high usage words ending in -**ay** and -**oy** (for example **days**, **boys**) which is correct, but also to high usage words where **y** should be changed to **i**, leading to typical errors such as **citys**, **partys**, **ponys**, **storys**, etc. Ideally teach the story below before any such errors become hand-habits (neuro motor patterns between hand and brain). These are very difficult to eradicate. Furthermore, the errors begin to 'look right' in the writer's eyes.

Play-acting is particularly useful for bringing home the **y**-**i** shift next to every new ending except **ing**.

The Yo-yo Man Changes Out of His Working Clothes

The Yo-yo Man really enjoys the work he does, finishing some words for Mr I and a great many words for Mr E. In fact, he has become a very familiar sight at the end of words. If, however, **ed**, **er**, **est** or any other ending (except -**ing**) comes along to finish the word for him, the Yo-yo Man stops work right away and changes out of his working clothes into some neat, straight **i**-clothes which Mr I has kindly given to him.

He keeps his **i**-clothes carefully folded in his **i**-pocket. You can sometimes see it on the trouser leg of his working clothes. The trousers of these **i**-clothes, however, are invisible, so that when the Yo-yo Man is working for Mr I he can even *look* like Mr I as well.

Anyone who observes carefully will see that the Yo-yo Man regularly disappears into his changing-hut to slip into his **i**-clothes in hundreds of words.

He hurries into the i-clothes which he carries.

cry, cries	fly, flies		enemy, enemies	
cries* allies	babies* parties*	armies centuries	enemies memories
flies* replies	cities* ponies	bodies cherries	fairies mysteries
tries* spies	countries* puppies*	beauties daisies	jellies studies
dries supplies	families* stories*	berries discoveries	ladies worries

* The starred words have priority in spelling.

Picture code each y changed to i

1. I like stories about puppies and ponies.
2. Those families have a lot of worries.

cry → cried   study → studied   reply → replied

cried	pried	allied	defied	justified	replied
dried	shield	amplified	denied	magnified	satisfied
fried	spied	applied	gratified	multiplied	signified
plied	tried	complied	horrified	occupied	supplied

accompanied	carried	jellied	studied
busied	emptied	married	tidied
buried	hurried	steadied	worried

Picture code each
y changed to i

1. They tried seeing how the fly looked when magnified.
2. She carried white roses when she got married.

angry → angrier   fly → flier   pretty → prettier

angrier	drier	flier	heavier	magnifier	steadier
busier	dustier	funnier	hungrier	merrier	sunnier
dirtier	easier	happier	lovelier	occupier	prettier

Picture code each
y changed to i

1. The occupier of the next house was angrier than I was.
2. When she felt happier she looked prettier than ever.

funny → funniest   ugly → ugliest

cloudiest	handiest	loveliest	pettiest	sandiest
greediest	laziest	moodiest	prettiest	speediest
hardiest	loneliest	muddiest	rustiest	spiciest

Picture code each y
and y changed to i

1. The shaggiest dog has the bushiest tail.
2. The friskiest pony has the silkiest coat.

-iness,	-iless,	-iful,	-ily,	-ihood,	-iment
business	tidiness	beautiful	busily	likelihood	merriment
happiness	penniless	merciful	easily	livelihood	envious
loneliness	merciless	plentiful	happily	embodiment	melodious

Picture code each y
and y changed to i

1. A busy business can bring happiness.
2. Her beauty lies in her beautiful eyes.

136

Take the time to make a folding changing hut so that the children can play-act the change. They go 'in' holding a **y** card, pretend to change, and emerge with the Yo-yo Man **i** card. Notice how **y** changes into i-clothes even when he has been working for Mr E, e.g. pon**y** -pon**ies**. Why? Because he hasn't got any **e**-clothes to change into!

Never Drop Y Before Adding -ing

The Yo-yo Man thinks it would look silly to change into his **i** clothes right beside an **i**. So he never changes clothes before -**ing**. Instead he finishes up the root word in his own working clothes usual. So don't drop him out!

crying	copying	carrying
drying	emptying	hurrying
flying	envying	marrying
frying	pitying	justifying
shying	studying	magnifying
spying	tidying	satisfying

Exception If a root word ends in **i** it is kept before **ing,** giving us a rare spectacle of two **i**'s in a row: e.g. sk**ii**ng, tax**ii**ng.

The Yo-yo Man Does Not Change His Clothes Before ay, oy and ey

When the Yo-yo Man is busy with the vowel behind him (out walking with a Vowel Man, or playing with Roy) he stays in his **y-** clothes.

play	delay	betray
played	delayed	betrays
player	way	betrayed
playful	wayward	betrayal
key	volley	journey
keys	volleys	journeys
keyed up	volleyed	journeyed
enjoy	annoy	employ
enjoyment	annoyed	employee
joyful	destroy	employment
	destroyer	

Note: Most **-ey** words end in **-key, -ley, -ney** (see page 104).

137

The Apple and the Witch

To a child who fails to develop a sight-vocabulary easily, reading a small word such as **saw** can be a real problem. Sounding out the letters only produces a non word, 'sss-ă-www'. Why isn't **a** saying 'ă'? Why isn't **w** saying '**www**'? The Picture Code

Card for **aw** and its story enables you to turn the moment when any child stumbles over the word **saw** or dr**aw**, etc. into an opportunity instead of a problem. Here is proof that the Witch's letter really spells trouble. (See also the **wh**, **ow**, **ew** and **wr** sections and **was**, **want,** etc. below.) Time your teaching of **aw** well apart from **ow** and **ew** to ensure that their sounds are not confused. Fortunately not many words contain the **aw** spelling pattern.

The Witch Makes the Apple Taste Awful

What happens to the **a**pple in words like s**aw**? Well, unfortunately the Wicked Water Witch loves fruit, especially **a**ppetising **a**pples. Whenever she discovers one of Mr A's **a**ppetising **a**pples behind her in a word she wants it for herself.

So she whirls round and tries to get the **a**pple out of its letter with a spelling spell. But . . .. no matter how hard she tries, none of her spells is powerful enough to get the **a**pple out. So she does something very wicked.

"If I cannot have it," she cries, "I won't let anyone else enjoy it either!" Then she splashes nasty spell water on to the **a**pple to make it taste **aw**ful. This is why, whenever you see an **a**pple and then the Wicked Water Witch in a word, the **a**pple will not be saying ă, as usual. Instead, you will hear an **aw** sound because the Witch has made it taste **aw**ful!

I saw her on the lawn at dawn.

awe	caw	draw	gnaw	lawn	prawn	shawl	tawny
awful	claw	drawing	hawk	lawyer	raw	spawn	thaw
awkward	crawl	drawl	hawthorn	outlaw	saw	sprawl	trawler
awning	dawdle	fawn	jaw	paw	scrawl	squawk	withdraw
brawn	dawn	flaw	law	pawn	seesaw	straw	yawn

**Picture code each
a, w and aw**

1. I saw the witch crawl across the lawn at dawn.
2. The hawk sat still and yawned.

My drawing

The Wicked
Water Witch
looks awful.
She has a
scrawny neck.
Michelle

Colouring for the Apples Tasting AWful When the children make their own dr**aw**ing of this pictogram, ask what colour(s) the **a**pple might be to show an **aw**ful taste. Brown? Purple? Blue? (Avoid black to make sure the letter stays dominant.) As you discuss it, repeat the word **aw**ful often. Make sure the children use it too, emphasizing the first syllable. And the **aw**ful-tasting liquid dripping off the broomstick? The same **aw**ful colour? Or another **aw**ful one? (If the suggestion arises that the liquid is poisonous, dismiss it. Letterland's Witch is not *that* bad!)

The Key Word is AWful If children remember the **a**pple as tasting "horrible" or "rotten", remind them that the key word is '**aw**ful', because **aw**ful holds the secret clue to the new sound. Let the children start their own collections of '**AW**ful Words'.

Play Act the AW Story Several children can be **a**pples bobbing happily up and down saying, "ă . . .,ă . . .,ă . . .". The Witch passes from left to right, turning back after each **a**pple. She holds out an imaginary broomstick and commands, "**A**pple, **a**pple, **a**pple, taste **aw**ful, **aw**ful, **aw**ful!" Each **a**pple responds by crying "**AW**!" in a contrasting tone of disappointment. Finally all **a**pples are moaning "**aw**" while the Witch shouts "**aw**" triumphantly. But as the Witch departs (in the Reading Direction), they all cheer up and start chanting "ă" again!

Why Can't the Witch Get the Apple if Other Letters Can? Some children will ask this question. If Giant **All** can grab as many **a**pples as he likes, and **Ar**thur **Ar** can steal them, why can't the **w**itch take them, too? The answer is: you have to be very clever to know how to get an **a**pple out of its own letter, and the Wicked Witch is not very clever. Too bad for her, but lucky for us. Otherwise she might cause even more trouble in words than she does already!

Other Irregularities Caused by W In numerous words such as **was, want, warm, war, worse, wonder, worm, forward, water** and **swan** the Witch's presence alters the sound of the vowel to the *right*, proving that she is almost as wicked to vowels on the *right* as to vowels to the *left*. Their new sounds, once she has 'spoilt' them, are so unpredictable that there are no pictograms for them. The best strategy is: beware of the Witch *wherever* you find her!

The Witch Makes the Apple Taste Awful From Underwater

When the Witch finds that she cannot get at any of Letterland's **a**ppetising **a**pples using spell water from her *own* letter she chases Uppy Umbrella away and fills *her* letter with water. Then she hides **u**nderwater and tries to get the **a**pple out with an **u**nderwater spell.

But her **u**nderwater spell is just as useless as ever. Furious, she makes the **a**pple taste **aw**ful again, as she has done before.

It is the naughty witch's fault.

applaud	author	cause	faucet	haughty	mauled	saunter
applause	authority	clause	fault	haunted	mausoleum	tarpaulin
applesauce	auto	cosmonaut	faulty	hydraulic	naughty	taught
astronaut	automatic	daub	fraud	jaunty	nautical	taunt
auburn	automobile	daughter	gaudy	launch	nauseating	taut
auction	autumn	daunting	gaunt	launderette	pause	undaunted
audience	caught	exhausted	haul	laundry	saucer	vault

Laura, Maude, Maureen, Paul, Pauline, August

> **Picture-code each
> a, u and au**

1. The faulty switch suddenly caused a fire.
2. Maude saw the astronaut who launched the rocket.

The **au** sound can be spelled in a least 10 different ways: **aw, au, or, ough, al, augh, ore, oar, oor** and **our**.

Mistakes like **sor** for **saw** and **cort** for **caught** are common, not to mention **work** for **walk**, and many others. It is best to make word collections and then group words spelt alike into funny phrases. Turn two large paintings of the **aw** and **au** pictograms into focal points. Display words with **aw**, **au** and **augh** under them.

For help with the four most common **augh** words try these two sentences about the Wicked Witch:

She **caught** her **naughty daughter** and slapped her. That **taught** her not to be so **naughty**!

More Vowel Men Out walking

Neither **ie** nor **ei** appears on the Vowel Men Out Walking scene because, unlike the other vowels, these pairs take turns with the talking. So the *first* vowel may be the silent look-out man. Since **ie** and **ei** also occur in fewer words than the other vowel pairs they are best introduced separately. The reverse side of the Picture Code Cards shows the second Vowel Man talking. By analysing the vowels' sound in any given word the children decide which side of the card appl**ie**s, and are guided by it when picture coding a word themselves. Colour *both* hollow letters yellow when Mr I's arm is up and *both* red when Mr E's arm is up. The *one* colour shows that between them they only make *one* sound.

When Mr I and Mr E Go Out Walking They Take Turns With The Talking

Mr I and Mr E both like walking and talking, so when *they* go out walking they take turns with the talking. They also take turns at being the look-out man. So sometimes the *first* one will be silent.

Have they tried this piece of pie?

allies	fried	amplified	satisfies	achieve	field	prairie	thieves
cried	lies	applies	simplified	brownie	grieve	retrieved	Annie
die	pie	justified	supplies	believe	niece	retriever	Grannie
flies	tied	magnified	terrified	briefcase	piece	shield	Jamie
				chief	pixie	thief	Stephanie

Never believe a lie.

Typical Mistakes   In the right hand list children frequently leave out the **i** or write **ei** by mistake. It helps if they make up their own sentences using these words, draw pictures to illustrate them and label all objects, e.g. The ch**ie**f saw the th**ie**f drop the sh**ie**ld in the f**ie**ld.

See also **ies** and **ied**, page 135.

When Mr E and I Go Out Walking They Take Turns With the Talking

ceiling	either
conceited	eiderdown
conceive	Fahrenheit
protein	height
receive	neither
seize	kaleidoscope

Picture code each ie and ie

1. His enemies tried to trick his allies.
2. I tied my golden retriever to a tree in the field.

Picture code each ei and ei

1. Did he receive the eiderdown we sent him?
2. Just when I had the kaleidoscope he seized it!

The Old Rule 'I Before E Except After C' This neat little rhyme is easy to 'parrot' but difficult to apply. Ask your children instead, "Which has the stronger Magic, **e** or **i**?" (They should answer **e**.) "Then expect Mr **E** to shoot the Blue Magic and change Clever Cat into a hissing snake." Therefore **c-e-i**, never **c-i-e**.

Why do We Hear 'a' in Words like 'Eight'?

Can you guess? Although he is very old and grey, in these few words Mr Mean-E goes out Walking! Kind Mr I acts as his silent look-out man even though Mr Mean-E is such an old grouch that he doesn't even d**ei**gn to smile. How old do you think Mr Mean-E might be? Golden Girl, who usually comes next in these words, has quietly decided that . . . .

...he must be eighty - eight !

eight	beige	neigh	weigh	rein
eighteen	deign	neighbour	weighty	feint
eighty	freight	reign	weightless	reindeer

More Vowels-Out-Walking Words to Picture Code:

green shield	shrieks and cries	piecemeal	magnified copies
fried beans	leave the fields	approaching thief	her niece's geese
sweet dreams	spied some grease	allies from the east	stealing pies

More About the Robbers

When Two Vowels Out Walking are Captured the Robber Does the Talking

Silent look-out men are not always able to spot a **r**obber in time to avoid being captured, so it is important to know what the wretched **r**obbers are up to. No Vowel Man can be expected to go on cheerfully saying his name when he has just been tossed into a **r**obber's sack! The **r**obbers usually shout out "**ear**" or "**air**" as they capture, except for **Or**vil **Or.**

a i r	o a r	e e r	e a r
aim but air fail but fair	boat but boar oats but oars	deep but deer bee but beer	eat but ear peach but pear

High Usage   Only the more frequent spelling patterns (**air** and **ear/-ear**) are provided on two Picture Code Cards.

Draw attention to **Arthur Ar**'s puff of hot **air** as he dashes off to his l**air**, and the 'air' and swollen **ear** details on the two sides of the **ear** card.

The other 'capture' pictograms are shown on the Robbers Flap Charts.   (See also page 112.)

In <u>here</u>, <u>there</u> and <u>where</u> the Surrounded Robber cries 'ear' or 'air'

What happens when **Er**nest **Er** is surrounded by **e**'s? In one word, **were**, he goes on saying '**er**' as usual, breaking Magic **e**'s wand to stop its sparks.

But in these three 'place' words, **Er**nest **Er** is unce**r**tain what to do. He is so ne**r**vous that he tries to ove**r**pow**er** them both at once. Finally he does,

		here
t		here
w		here

but not until Mr E and his twin have landed a few punches on his ear first. Perhaps this is why the **r**obber goes off crying 'ear' in the word **here**. In **there** and **where** he puffs out hot 'air', probably because two vowel men are heavy to carry!

Now, where shall I hide, here? there? where?

Lazy Robbers Do Not Steal

Robbers do not always behave as you might expect them to. Sometimes they feel lazy. Then they cannot be bothered to steal the vowel.

c a r but c a r avan

her but her itage

for but for est

barbarian	parish	perish	florist	foreign	spirit
paragraph	parallel	periscope	forest	orange	miracle

Carol, Clara, Clarence, Harold, Marion, Marianne, Doris, Dorothy, Florence, Gerald, Geraldine, Jeremy, Terence, Teresa, America.

Robbers Often Trick the Witch as They Steal

No **r**obber likes to be watched by the Witch when he is stealing. So when she is there they often say a different **r**obber's name or mutter **'uh'** as they steal, just to confuse her.

 wo r ds towa r ds backwa r ds

award	swarm	thwart	ward	warm	warn	warp	wart
reward	toward	thwarted	warden	warmth	warning	warped	wardrobe
	backward	forward	inward	outward	Edward	Howard	
word	work	workshop	worldly	wormy	worry	worst	worth
wordless	worker	world	worm	worried	worse	worship	worthless

Racing Robbers Rarely Rob.

Racing Robbers drop their loads so that they can race each other whenever they meet in a word. Often they are also protecting a vowel from a Magic Ending's sparks. They are really behaving like Best Friends to the rescue, but only accidentally. All they are interested in is the chance to run a race!

barrel	marriage	errand	terror	irresistible	horrid	currant
carry	narrow	ferry	terrible	squirrel	horror	current
carrot	parrot	herring	mirror	borrow	sorry	furrow
carriage	sparrow	Jerry	irritate	lorry	sorrow	hurry
marry	berry	merry	irregular	horrible	tomorrow	turret

What's Happened to the Apple?

What has happened to the **a** in f**a**ther? How can we explain to an exasperated young speller why father spelt f**a**rther is wrong, and also f**a**rst (f**a**st) and p**a**rst (p**a**st) etc? In Letterland the question becomes "What's happened to the **a**pple?" The answer is

"Guess what! You have discovered a Yawning Apple!" These **a**pples are rare in some regions and frequent in others, depending on accent.

At a later date the question should arise, "What's happened to the **a**pple in words like Indi**a** and **A**meric**a**?" That is another story! Each story sharpens your children's listening skills.

Make each **a** the focus of a word collection. Let everyone invent sentences to link examples to each other.

Yawning Apples Say 'Ah'

Most **a**pples say "ă" for ăpple in words (unless they are unlucky enough to be stolen). But in some words apples get sleepy. Just as they are about to say "ă" they start to yawn. With their mouths so wide open their usual ă sound comes out as "ah".

Look, glass on the grass!

after	blast	daft	grant	mast	plant	rather
Amen	brass	dance	grass	master	plaster	slant
answer	calf	father	half	nasty	prance	tomato
ask	cast	France	headmaster	past	quality	wand
basket	class	glass	last	pasture	quantity	wander

Picture code each a and yawning apple
1. The calf ran after my father.
2. Ask her for the answer at half past nine.

Parachuted Apples Say "Uh"

Many names of far away countries end with an **a**pple letter. But these **a**pples make an 'ŭ' sound, as in ŭmbrella! Why? Well, these **a**pples need to be transported to the far away countries by air. Since Mr A has no plane he has solved his delivery problem by parachuting them in, each with the help of one of Mr U's **u**mbrellas. As the **a**pple lands it *tries* to say 'ă' as usual but the only sound that comes out is "ŭ" because it lands with such a thud! Mr A also uses parachuted apples for 'rush jobs' closer to home.

Africa   Asia   America   umbrella

Africa	Asia	Canada	Malaysia	b**a**nan**a**	car**a**van
Algeria	Austria	China	Tunisia	camer**a**	canv**a**s
America	Australia	India	Russia	gorill**a**	cat**a**pult
Arabia	Burma	Libya	Yugoslavia	umbrell**a**	par**a**chute

Odd Beginnings

There are quite a few instances in the English language where either the first or the second letter in a word is silent, e.g. **wh** as in **when**, **wr** as in **write**, **ch** as in **choir**, **kn** as in **know** plus **gn**, **ps**, **rh** and **mn**. The last three are too infrequent to warrant a story. The gn story itself has low teaching priority, but may amuse the otherwise frustrated speller.

The Golden Girl Suddenly Feels All Shy next to Nick

When Naughty Nick and Golden Girl are face to face in a word they usually si**ng** together. But when they are back to back in a word (so that they cannot see each other) Golden Girl suddenly feels all shy. Because she does not know what to say, she just says nothing. This is why you cannot hear her in these words.

She saw a gnat on the sign.

gnat	gnaw	gnu	foreign	resign
gnarled	gnawed	benign	malign	sign
gnash	gnome	campaign	reign	sovereign

Blushing (This pictogram is not on a Picture Code Card or Chart.) If children wish to draw their own versions of for **gn** they can colour Golden Girl's face bright red to show that she is blushing with shyness.

Exceptions Occasionally she overcomes her shyness. Then she says "**g** . . ." for Golden Girl as usual, e.g. i**g**nore, si**g**nature.

sign

but

signal

Other Silent Consonants The general strategy, with any two *unusual* initial consonants should be: assume that either one could be silent, e.g. **ps** in **p**sychology, **rh** in **r**hinoceros, **mn** in **m**nemonic, **pn** in **pn**eumonia.

146

Odd Endings

Since the -**ture** ending is often pronounced "chuh" (as in pic**ture**) it is easily misread and mis-spelt **c-h e-r**. The only high usage word actually spelt -**cher** is tea**cher**. By contrast over 40 useful words end in -**ture**. So a rough and ready rule for the **cher** sound is: unless the word is tea**cher**, use **t-u-r-e**. Leave time between teaching **ture** and **tion**. Give -**tion** priority since -**tion** makes a far larger number of seemingly 'too long' words easy to read and spell.

This section also explains the 'odd' sound of **qu** in the suffix - **que**, and other odd endings.

Ticking Tom Sneezes as Urgent Ur Breaks Magic E's Wand

As **Ur**gent **Ur** runs past Ticking Tom he hears a sound just like Clever Cat sneezing, '**ch**!' But Clever Cat is nowhere to be seen. "So who sneezed?" wonders **Ur**gent **Ur** as he rushes past Tom, crying '**ur**!' "Could it be Ticking Tom?" Yes, it is!

Notice how **Ur**gent **Ur** always overpowers the Magic **e** at the end to make sure it can't turn his stolen **u**mbrella into a Vowel Man!

Who will venture to capture Urgent Ur?

architecture	departure	gesture	moisture	premature	stature
capture	feature	lecture	nature	puncture	temperature
caricature	fixture	literature	overture	rapture	texture
creature	furniture	mature	picture	sculpture	torture
culture	future	mixture	posture	signature	venture

Picture code each ch and ture

1. He watched the wild creatures of nature.
2. Do you like the texture of this furniture?

The Queen Makes Trouble in the -que Ending

Normally you would expect the Quarrelsome Queen to say "**qu**" as usual in this ending. Instead, just to be difficult, she makes Clever Cat's little '**c** . . .' sound instead. She has even silenced Mr **U** and **E** out walking. What an impossible queen! (This pictogram is not shown on a Picture Code Card.)

She won't queue up to pay by cheque.

antique	grotesque	oblique	picturesque	statuesque
cheque	Monique	opaque	plaque	technique
brusque	critique	mosque	physique	unique

anti**que**

Cover the **q**ueen's hair to make -**que** look like **c**! Notice too how Mr I squeaks '**e**' when he has to be face to face with her!

-Less and -ness take Double S

-Less and -ness take double-s.

Once you know that this is so, If you forget the second **s** in -**ness** or -**less**, it's simply

carelessness!

-less

unless	shapeless	senseless
timeless	tasteless	meaningless
toothless	wireless	worthless
lifeless	harmless	valueless
motherless	speechless	stainless
blameless	priceless	pointless

-ness

illness	dampness	fairness
sickness	darkness	brightness
goodness	stiffness	shyness
kindness	fondness	willingness
sadness	loudness	selfishness
likeness	deafness	politeness

-lessness

uselessness	hopelessness	sleeplessness
helplessness	lawlessness	shamelessness
restlessness	heedlessness	endlessness

One n for the root word, one for -ness

thinness	drunkenness
evenness	stubbornness

Munching Mike Takes Ben's Breath Away

When Munching Mike murmurs "Mmmm" right behind Bouncy Ben's back, he takes Bouncy Ben's breath away! That is why no one can hear him at the end of these words.

climb	comb	plumbing	crumb(s)
limb	bomb	plumber	dumb
lamb	bomber	thumb	numb

Make as short a sentence as possible from each group of words. Other examples: breadcru**mb**s, co**mb**, honeyco**mb**. Less common: aplo**mb**, to**mb**, wo**mb**, succu**mb**.

Apart from these words -**mb** is rare. Bouncy Ben, it seems keeps well away from Munching Mike most of the time!

Munching Mike and Naughty Nick

Munching Mike also takes Naughty Nick's breath away, but only in these few words:

autumn	condemn	column
damn	hymn	solemn

Clearly Naughty Nick does not like getting too near Munching Mike either!

autumn

Mr 'Tion's Tea Parties

Your first rea**ction** to this se**ction** may be, 'Oh, I won't need to men**tion** words with **-tion** for a long time . If so, you should ques**tion** your posi**tion**. Listen to Mr **'Tion's** conversa-**tion** in Songbook 2B. Many **-tion** words carry important informa**tion**. They are also great confidence boosters. Children feel good when they can read a word as long as telecommunica**tion** – and even spell it too!
Any child who memorises this story's title should be able to read and spell **-tion** correctly in over 1,500 words. Children prone to writing **-shon, -shun** or **-toin** might like to know that none of these spellings ever occurs, not even in *one* English word! However a few do end in **-sion**.

Mr 'Tion Says " . . ... Tea I Owe Nick"

Have you ever met a teacher called Mr **'Tion**? He teaches reading and spelling at Naughty Nick's school. Everybody likes Mr **'Tion** because he often gives **t**ea parties.

One day Mr **'Tion** gave a **t**ea party for all of Nick's class. Before serving tea he asked everybody to spell some easy words and then some harder words. Everyone did quite well, so he was pleased. Then he said, "I think I know a word which you can't spell; my name, **'Tion**!" By then Nick was getting thirsty. He was sure he knew how to spell Mr **'Tion**'s name. So he said, "Let's say that whoever spells Mr **'Tion**'s name right first will be served tea first."

"All right," Mr **'Tion** agreed. Many children tried to spell **tion** but they all started with **sh**, which is wrong. Then Nick said *he* would try. "What's more," he said to Mr **'Tion**, "I'll bet that after I whisper the right spelling for **tion** into your ear, the first thing you say will show everyone *else* how to spell **tion**." "How can that be?" everyone asked. Mr **'Tion** called out "**sh** . . ." so that he could hear Nick whispering.

Then Mr **'Tion** smiled. He poured Nick's tea and said, "Here's the **T**ea **I O**we **N**ick". So now all of the children remember how to spell **-tion** by saying to themselves what Mr **'Tion** said to Nick at the party: "..the **T**ea **I O**we **N**ick".

Please

pay attention

to words which mention Mr. 'Tion's name.

action	attention	correction	instructions	objection	question
addition	caution	destruction	intention	perfection	repetition
adoption	condition	fiction	introduction	portion	section
affection	construction	fraction	invention	position	subscription
ammunition	contraption	infection	mention	prevention	subtraction

Picture code each t, th and tion

1. His instructions were to make three corrections.
2. Did Judith mention an objection to Tom's invention?

Mr A Says His Name Whenever He Comes to One of Mr 'Tion's Tea Parties

One of Mr **'Tion**'s closest friends is Mr A. So Mr A has a standing invit**ation** to all of Mr **'Tion**'s tea parties. Mr A loves going to parties so you will often hear him saying his name as he arrives at Mr **'Tion**'s house. Can you hear him saying "**a**!" beside Mr **'Tion** in these words?

His destin**ation** is Mr. **'Tion**'s house.

aviation	destination	imagination	limitation	sensation
combination	explanation	information	operation	station
complication	exploration	investigation	population	translation
conversation	foundation	hesitation	relation	transportation

Picture code each tion and ation

1. They took action to prevent starvation.
2. This translation has a questionable interpretation.

Roughly 1000 out of 1500 **-tion** words end in **-ation**! Place your Mr A card beside your **tion** card to display these words. Young writers won't shy away from them once they are confident of their spelling.

Other Vowel Men Also Say Their Names as They Join Mr 'Tion

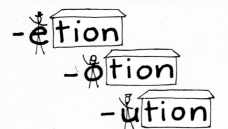

Sometimes other Vowel Men come to see Mr **'Tion** when he is having a tea party. When they do come, they always say their name as they arrive at his house.

I won a prom**otion** because of my sol**ution**.

completion	lotion	notion	contribution	institution	resolution
devotion	locomotion	promotion	evolution	persecution	revolution
emotion	motion	constitution	execution	solution	substitution

150

Mr I Just Leaves Some Ink for Mr 'Tion

Mr **'Tion** likes to make all of the Vowel Men feel welcome at his tea parties, but Mr I finds it embarrassing to be invited because he does not like tea. So he just brings a bottle of **i**nk as a little gift, apologises for not staying, and hurries away. This is why all words with **i** before **-tion** say "**ition**", and none of them say "**ītion**".

Mr. I is in a difficult posi[tion].

addition	composition	expedition	nutrition	repetition
ambition	definition	exhibition	position	superstition
ammunition	demolition	ignition	proposition	tradition
competition	edition	imposition	recognition	transition

In Summary: Every Vowel Man says his name before -tion except Mr I.

-ā[tion] -ē[tion] -ō[tion] -ū[tion]

but -ĭ[tion]

> **Picture code each -ātion, -ētion, -ition, -ōtion and -ūtion**

On completion of the Christmas celebrations, and when the commotion was over, we made New Year resolutions because that was the tradition.

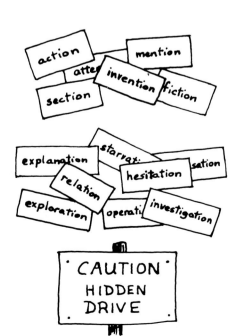

Practice With -tion and -ation Words   Children usually expect long words to be much harder to read than short ones. By keeping a look out for **-tion** and **-ation** endings in long words they dispel this fear and soon learn to take an overview of *any* longer word. So it is worth spending time on the **-tion** endings.

Make a set of **-tion** and **-ation** cards. Use them for an easy Kim's Game (find two **-tion** or two **-ation** words when all are face down). Later add more cards with **-etion**, **-otion** and -**-ution** words. Include scoring, giving the last three a higher value than the more common **-tion** and **-ation** words.

Children often find it easier at first to work back from the end of a **-tion** word.

investigation
" . . . . . . .tion
 . . . . .ātion
 . . . . . . .gation
inves . . . .
investigation"

institution
" . . . . . .tion
 . . . . . .ūtion
 . . . . .tution
insti . . . . . .
institution"

151

Words Ending in sion.

-sion

When words end in **-sion** you can often tell that the spelling will not be **tion** by their pronunciation. While **-tion** starts with a voice*less* 'sh' we say '**zhon**' in **-sion**, by adding voice to the 'sh' sound.

collision	delusion	explosion	occasion	seclusion
conclusion	diversion	fusion	persuasion	supervision
confusion	division	illusion	precision	transfusion
conversion	erosion	intrusion	provision	version
decision	excursion	invasion	revision	vision

-ssion

But these **-sion** words are pronounced exactly like **-tion**. Most end in **-ssion**. An odd one out: cu**shion**.

concussion	expression	percussion	profession	dimension
confession	impression	permission	session	pension
depression	mission	possession	succession	propulsion
discussion	passion	procession	expansion	tension

The 'shal' sound at the End of Words

tial

cial

Over 45 English words sound as though they end in **-shal**. Yet only one is spelt with **shal** (mar**shal**). Over 30 end in **tial** and more than 15 in **cial**. The most useful of these are listed below. The **sh** sound in **tial** is the same as that in **tion** words. A little trick for remembering the **cial** spelling: draw a shadowy **sh** around **ci**. The **al** part of these two endings means 'to do with' (see page 133).

This spe**cial** inform**ation** is not essen**tial**.

				Also -cian	
confidential	initial	artificial	official		
differential	partial	commercial	racial	electrician	musician
essential	potential	crucial	social	magician	optician
influential	spatial	financial	special	mathematician	politician

Picture code or box each ti and ci saying 'sh'

1. The initial shipment of timber was substantial.
2. Our Musician's Club organised this social event.

The '...us' Words

Low visualisers predictably omit the silent **o** when spelling **-ous**. Reduce errors by giving them the odds, roughly 16 to 1, in favour of **ous**! Talk about the '**us**' ending instead of the '**o-u-s**' ending so that, even if they never become skilled at analysing Describing Words or at remembering that **ous** usually means 'full of', they will still be on the alert. If, coming to a word 'ear first', they hear themselves saying 'fam...**us**', 'mountain...**us**', etc. their strategy should be, 'when in doubt, don't leave Mr O out!' Once they have learnt the few high usage words that really do end in **us** (circ**us**, etc.) the odds are even greater in favour of **o-u-s**. Suggest that each child makes an **ous** collection called 'Numer**ous** Describing Words'. It will be a useful personal resource in their free writing.

Mr O Becomes Breathless in Describing Words which End in -ous

Many Describing Words end in **o-u-s**. (An **-ous** ending usually means 'full of'.) But...you will never hear Mr O in those words, even though you can see his letter. Why not? Because Mr O is 'so full' of excitement about the things being described that he can hardly speak. Describing Words (adjectives and adverbs) it seems, just take his breath away! Over 235 useful Describing Words end in **o-u-s**, so whenever you want to spell a Describing Word, do not forget to put Mr O in there, breathlessly silent before the '...**us**'" ending.

These describing words are fabul*ous*.

adventurous	frivolous	marvellous	outrageous	strenuous
boisterous	generous	miraculous	perilous	stupendous
covetous	glamorous	mischievous	poisonous	thunderous
dangerous	gorgeous	momentous	pompous	treacherous
disastrous	hazardous	monstrous	prosperous	tremendous
enormous	hideous	murderous	ravenous	vigorous
fabulous	humorous	nervous	ridiculous	virtuous

Take Care If a word ending in **-us** is *not* a describing word (e.g. asparag**us**, cact**us**, circ**us**, croc**us**, fung**us**, hippopotam**us**, min**us**, vir**us**, walr**us**) Mr O will not be there. Draw and label these words. There are not many others without **o** before **us**. So after that, if in doubt *don't* leave Mr O out.

> **Picture code each ous**

1. That enormous elephant is not dangerous.
2. One tremendously good idea made her famous.

An i Before -ous May Sound Like e

Many of the describing words which end in **-o-u-s** are preceded by **i**. Often it will be the Yo-yo Man changed into his **i**-clothes. Although he wears his **i**-clothes he may sound as though he is working for Mr E! In three or four words there really will be an **e**! (You will find this on a Flap Chart and on **i** and **ous** Picture Code Cards.)

serious   studious

-ious	envious	harmonious	luxurious	studious	**-eous**	courageous
	furious	hilarious	melodious	various		gorgeous
	glorious	industrious	mysterious	victorious		hideous

Picture code each -ious

1. It is obvious that he is ingenious.
2. I am anxious that he will become curious.

Ti- and ci- sound like sh before -ous

Since you have met Mr '**Tion** you know that **ti** can sound like **sh**, as in Mr '**Tion**'s name. When **tion** words are changed into Describing Words (e.g. infec**tion**/infec**tious**) in rushes breathless Mr O before **-us**. So the new '**shus**' sound is spelt **ti-ous**. Not one English word ends in **-shus**.

A few Describing Words are spelt **ci-ous** instead of **ti-ous**, especially if the last consonant in the root word is **c**. The two groups of **-tious** and **-cious** words listed below are the most useful '**shus**' words to know how to spell.

This food is both nutritious and delicious.

ambitious		precious	
-tious	ambitious infectious	**-cious**	conscious officious
	cautious nutritious		delicious spacious
	fictitious repetitious		gracious suspicious
	flirtatious superstitious		precious vicious

154

The -able/-ible Endings

Since neither **i** nor **a** say their names in **ible** and **able** the Candle Magic is shown as out of action. The vowel in these suffixes is not stressed. The resulting pronunciation of both **ible** and **able** in words such as terr**ible** and wash**able** (and most other **ible** and **able** words) is virtually identical: "ŭ-ble". The child who searches for a sound-clue to help him to decide which to write does not find one.

The following guidelines are provided for children who are ready to learn some rules set out in more conventional terms.

Whole-Words Take the Whole-Word Ending: -able

Since the word 'able' is a whole-word in its own right this rule is really a case of one whole-word being combined with another whole-word. It has its counterpart in 'Part-Words Take the Part-Word Ending: **-ible**' (see below).

acceptable	considerable	mentionable	profitable	suitable
available	drinkable	obtainable	punishable	variable
avoidable	fashionable	payable	questionable	understandable
bearable	marketable	perishable	reasonable	washable
breakable	mendable	predictable	sinkable	workable

Whole-Words Minus e Take -able

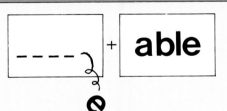

If the root word still sounds like a whole-word when pronounced with its "u-ble" ending but the silent **e** at the end is dropped (because the new ending begins with a vowel), that new ending will be **-able** just like the whole-words listed above.

advisable	consumable	desirable	excitable	movable
arguable	curable	dispensable	excusable	notable
believable	debatable	disposable	forgivable	reputable
conceivable	deplorable	disputable	lovable	valuable

155

Root Words Which Can Be Made to End in -ation Take -able

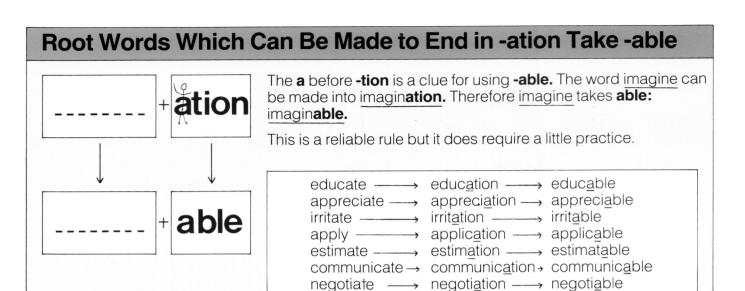

The **a** before **-tion** is a clue for using **-able.** The word imagine can be made into imagin**ation**. Therefore imagine takes **able:** imagin**able.**

This is a reliable rule but it does require a little practice.

educate ⟶	education ⟶	educable
appreciate ⟶	appreciation ⟶	appreciable
irritate ⟶	irritation ⟶	irritable
apply ⟶	application ⟶	applicable
estimate ⟶	estimation ⟶	estimatable
communicate →	communication →	communicable
negotiate ⟶	negotiation ⟶	negotiable

Hard c or g Words Take -able

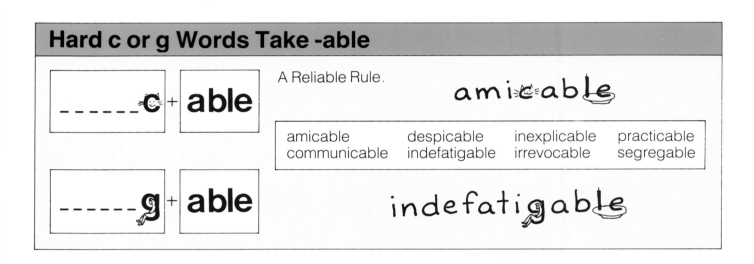

A Reliable Rule.

amicable

amicable	despicable	inexplicable	practicable
communicable	indefatigable	irrevocable	segregable

indefatigable

If Silent e Is Not Dropped Use -able

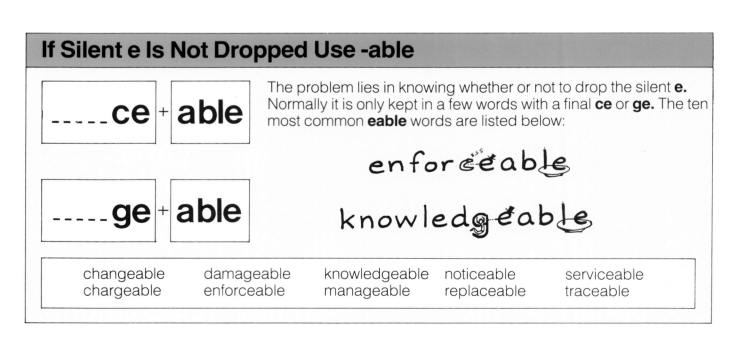

The problem lies in knowing whether or not to drop the silent **e.** Normally it is only kept in a few words with a final **ce** or **ge.** The ten most common **eable** words are listed below:

enforceable

knowledgeable

changeable	damageable	knowledgeable	noticeable	serviceable
chargeable	enforceable	manageable	replaceable	traceable

Part-Words Take the Part-Word Ending -ible

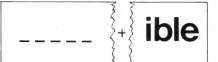

If the root of the word is not a whole-word when pronounced alone, it will usually take **ible**.

terrible

compat . . .compatible	feas . . .feasible	suscept . . .susceptible
divis . . .divisible	horr . . .horrible	vis . . .visible
ed . . . .edible	terr . . .terrible	invis . . .invisible

However, some whole words also take **ible** because they follow the next rule.

Words Ending in -tion and -sion Take -ible

The **-tion** words must be distinguished from **-ation** words. Where there is no **a** in front of **-tion** or **-sion** use **-ible**.

combustion – combustible	compression – compressible
corruption – corruptible	division – divisible
destruction – destruct i ble	impression – impressible
exhaustion – inexhaustible	omission – omiss i ble
perception –imperceptible	permission – permissible

Soft c and g Words Take -ible

In most words the **e** in a final **ce** or **ge** is dropped in favour of the **ible** ending to keep **c** or **g** soft. This is a more sensible solution to the problem than the clumsy looking **eable.**

coercible	eligible	irascible	negligible
crucible	illegible	intelligible	reducible
dirigible	incorrigible	invincible	tangible

But note: forcible, but enforceable!

Exploring Words Round the World

EXPLORING WORDS IN DIFFERENT PARTS OF THE WORLD. Since the spelling of names of places and their pronunciation do not always congrue, exceptions must be expected when searching for letter-people in geography vocabulary. Nevertheless a look at a map of the world shows straight away that most of the robbers are world travellers, for a start, and that the vowel men turn up in a wide variety of places, distance not withstanding.

ARthur AR feels very much at home in **Denmark, Argentina** and the **Antarctic,** (and even on **Mars!**). ORvil OR loves the **North,** especially **Norway,** but is also happy in **New York** or **Singapore.** IRving IR is not a keen traveller, but URgent UR likes **Burma** and **Turkey,** while ERnest ER's longer legs take him rapidly from **Germany** to **Switzerland** into the **Mediterranean** and across numerous **Deserts.**

A favourite spot for vowels out walking is the **East Coast** of **Spain,** but they also enjoy the coasts of **Greenland, New Zealand** and **Greece,** and the **Plains** of the **Ukraine.** (They are particularly fond of travelling to these places by **Sea**.) Mr I shows an individual preference for **China,** Mr O is very fond of **Poland, Mexico** and the **Congo.** Mr U prefers **Cuba** and **Portugal,** while Mr E finds **Indonesia, Sweden** and **Egypt** all fascinating places to be.

Furthermore, Mr E has arranged for Magic E's to give vowel men friends a chance to appear in the **United States, Iceland, Ireland** and **Wales,** and on great rivers like the **Danube,** and **Nile** and the **Rhine,** to go out into numerous beautiful **Lakes,** some big, famous cities like **Rome,** and even as far as the North and South **Pole.** Unfortunately his magic sparks burn out in the **Philippines.**

Taken all in all, the Letterland people do get about in the world. Have a look for yourself. Look into the number of countries where other Letterland people go. In which countries or cities, for example, can you expect to find Gentle Ginger, the Gymnast performing in international competitions?

Mediterranean Sea

Over to the Children

You can elicit new Letterland logic from the children once they have come to expect a Letterland explanation for most new words. Expect them to seize on any irregularity and ask "What's the story for this one?" But Letterland explanations are limited to *recurring* spelling patterns. So for any 'one-off' word for which this Teacher's Guide give you no story, it's over to the children to think up their own explanation! Tell them that the whole Letterland System began because one child invented the **aw** story.

Samples of particularly good explanations thought up by children:

Homonym Problem Solved   How can you tell when to write **sure** or **shore**?   And why can't we see that the Hat Man is hushing up Sammy Snake in the word **sure**? The answer: you can be **sure** that the Hairy Hat Man will always be away at the sea**shore!**

How can the 'fff' sound in *laugh* and *cough* be explained? For **laugh** a 7-year old girl offered this suggestion: Golden Girl tickles the Hairy Hat Man's bare feet with a feather to make him lau**gh**, just in the word **laugh**. He hates noise so he stifles his lau**gh**, making a **'fff'** sound.

Quite independently in another school 6 year olds thought that both Golden Girl and the Hairy Hat Man have cou**gh**s in the word **cough.** They decided that trying to stifle a **rough,tough cough** would cause the **'fff'** sound which seems reasonable **enough.**

Maybe your children can think of a good Letterland reason for the silent **u** in g**u**ide and g**u**itar, or the shift from **f** to **v** in wi**f**e, wi**v**es, etc.

Even if no one comes up with a very good story, the time spent thinking about the words which contain these anomalies is actually helping weak spellers to start getting these words right in future, and to realise that correct spelling is important.

Alphabetical Index